DIGITAL MARKETING ANALYTICS

THE DATA BEHIND DIGITAL

ANUSHKA, SWATI SINGH

To the curious minds who seek clarity in a world of data.
To the marketers who believe that insight drives impact.
And to every analyst, student, and strategist turning numbers into narratives—
this book is for you.

Contents

Foreword

In today's hyperconnected digital landscape, marketing is no longer guided by instinct alone—it is powered by data, shaped by algorithms, and refined through continuous measurement. The shift from creative storytelling to data-driven decision-making has transformed the way organizations reach, engage, and retain their audiences. Digital Marketing Analytics arrives at a pivotal moment when marketers are being challenged not only to create compelling messages but to prove their effectiveness in quantifiable ways.

This book serves as both a roadmap and a resource for navigating the complex ecosystem of digital data. It bridges the gap between marketing theory and real-world application, offering readers a practical framework to analyze performance across channels, optimize campaigns, and make data-backed strategic decisions. From web analytics to social media metrics, from mobile insights to attribution modeling—this work covers the critical pillars of a modern digital analytics strategy.

Whether you're a student stepping into the field, a professional seeking to sharpen your analytical edge, or an executive leading digital transformation, this book equips you with the tools to turn data into action. It emphasizes not just what to measure, but why it matters—and how to translate metrics into meaningful marketing outcomes.

As digital platforms continue to evolve and consumer behaviors shift with unprecedented speed, the ability to interpret and act on data is no longer optional. It is essential. Digital Marketing Analytics empowers its readers to embrace that challenge with clarity, confidence, and purpose.

Preface

In today's data-driven world, successful digital marketing is built not on guesswork, but on insight. Digital Marketing Analytics: The Data Behind Digital equips students, educators, and professionals with the foundational tools and analytical techniques essential to thrive in modern marketing environments.

This textbook offers a comprehensive yet accessible introduction to digital marketing analytics. From understanding key performance metrics to leveraging tools like Google Analytics, social media insights, and customer journey mapping, this book bridges the gap between marketing theory and real-world data application. Core concepts such as customer segmentation, campaign tracking, A/B testing, and ROI measurement are explained with clarity, supported by real examples and practical case studies.

Whether you're new to the field or looking to sharpen your analytical edge, this book is your essential guide to making smarter, data-informed marketing decisions in the digital age.

Acknowledgements

Writing Digital Marketing Analytics has been a journey of research, reflection, and collaboration—and it would not have been possible without the support and contributions of many individuals and institutions.

First and foremost, I would like to express my deep gratitude to my mentors, colleagues, and students who inspired many of the questions and insights explored in this book. Their enthusiasm for the ever-evolving world of digital marketing and their pursuit of clarity in data-driven decision-making provided constant motivation.

To the professionals in the field—marketers, analysts, strategists, and educators—who shared their experiences, case studies, and feedback during the development of this book, thank you for grounding theory in real-world practice.

Special thanks are due to Dr. Durgesh Singh, Assistant Consultant at Tata Consultancy Services. His insightful guidance, timely encouragement, and technical input played a vital role in making this book possible. His support was instrumental throughout the editorial process.

A special thank you to the academic community and industry experts whose work laid the foundation for many of the frameworks and best practices discussed throughout these pages.

I am also grateful to my editorial and publishing team for their guidance, patience, and belief in this project. Their commitment to quality and clarity made this book what it is.

Finally, to my family and close friends—thank you for your unwavering support, encouragement, and understanding through long hours of writing and research. Your belief in me means everything.

This book is the result of collective knowledge, collaboration, and continuous learning. To all who contributed, directly or indirectly, I am sincerely thankful.

Prologue

We live in a world flooded with digital noise—billions of emails, social media posts, ads, videos, and searches exchanged daily. Every click, scroll, and swipe leaves behind a data trail. Hidden within that trail is a story: the story of how people engage, what they value, and why they act. Digital Marketing Analytics is the art and science of uncovering that story.

This book begins at the intersection of two worlds—marketing and data. One is driven by creativity and storytelling; the other, by precision and patterns. Together, they form the backbone of modern marketing strategy. Today's marketers are no longer judged solely on creativity but on results: engagement, conversions, retention, and return on investment. And to achieve those results, they must become fluent in the language of data.

The purpose of this book is not to overwhelm you with numbers or jargon but to make sense of the metrics that matter. From tracking website traffic to decoding social media trends, from understanding user journeys to optimizing content performance, this book offers the tools to transform data into direction.

The digital landscape changes rapidly. Algorithms update, platforms rise and fall, and consumer behavior evolves. But what remains constant is the need to understand your audience—deeply, authentically, and accurately. That understanding now comes through analytics.

Whether you are a student eager to enter the field, a professional refining your skillset, or a business leader making strategic decisions, this book is your companion in navigating the dynamic world of digital marketing with clarity and confidence.

Welcome to Digital Marketing Analytics. Let's turn data into insight—and insight into action.

CHAPTER ONE

Introduction to Digital Marketing Analytics

1.1 What is Digital Marketing Analytics?

Digital Marketing Analytics is the practice of collecting, analyzing, and interpreting data from digital marketing efforts to guide decision-making and strategy. It involves tracking metrics from digital platforms like websites, social media, email, and search engines to evaluate campaign performance and customer behavior.

In an age where data is abundant, analytics transforms raw numbers into actionable insights. It empowers marketers to measure the effectiveness of campaigns, understand customer journeys, personalize content, and optimize marketing ROI.

Components of Digital Marketing Analytics

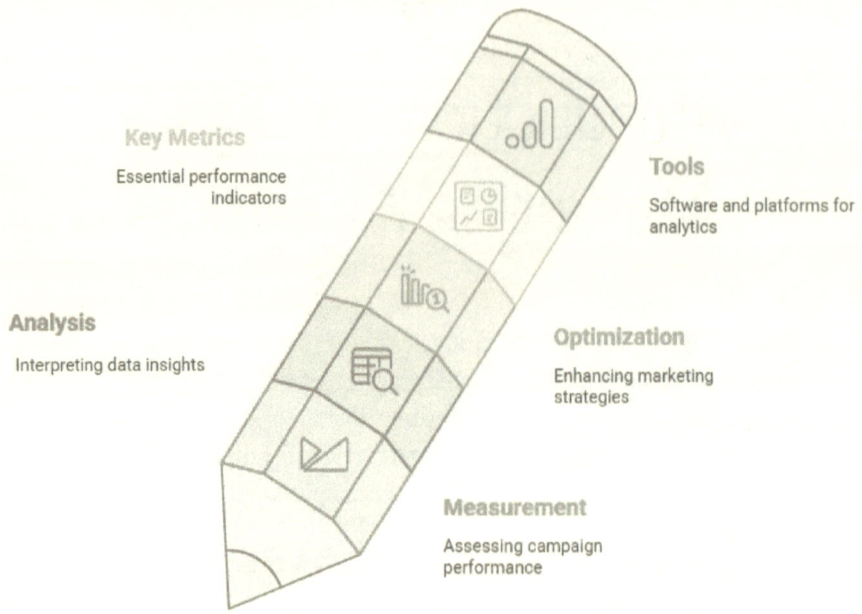

1.2 The Evolution of Marketing Analytics

Marketing analytics has come a long way from its early roots in traditional advertising. In the past, marketing success was gauged through broad indicators such as TV ratings, print circulation, or general sales lift. Decisions were largely based on experience, intuition, and limited consumer research, which offered only a fragmented view of customer behavior. However, the emergence of digital technologies radically changed this landscape. The introduction of Customer Relationship Management (CRM) systems in the 1980s and 1990s marked the first major shift toward data-driven marketing, allowing businesses to capture and analyze customer interactions in more structured ways. This gave rise to targeted campaigns, personalized messaging, and basic metrics like response rates and customer lifetime value.

The real transformation occurred with the digital revolution of the 2000s. As websites, search engines, email, and social media platforms gained traction, marketers were suddenly equipped with a wealth of real-time data. Analytics evolved from static reports to dynamic dashboards, enabling marketers to measure impressions, clicks, conversions, bounce rates, and more—all in real time. Multichannel tracking became possible, allowing a better understanding of how users move between platforms and devices. Today, with advancements in artificial intelligence, big data, and predictive analytics, marketing has become more precise, personalized, and performance-oriented than ever before. What was once driven by gut feeling is now governed by data, making analytics an essential foundation of modern marketing strategy.

Marketing has come a long way from the days of intuition and guesswork. Here's a brief timeline:

- **Pre-Digital Era:** In the Pre-Digital Era, marketing decisions were primarily driven by professional experience, consumer surveys, and traditional media metrics. Marketers relied on their intuition and long-term industry knowledge to guide strategies, supported by insights from focus groups, in-person interviews, and mailed questionnaires. Media planning was based on broad audience data from sources like TV ratings, radio listenership, and print circulation figures. Without real-time data, campaign effectiveness was assessed through delayed sales reports and retailer feedback, making it difficult to quickly adapt strategies or measure precise ROI.
- **Web 1.0 (Static Web):** During the Web 1.0 era, also known as the Static Web, marketing entered the digital space with limited interactivity and basic tracking capabilities. Websites functioned primarily as online brochures, offering static content with minimal user engagement. Marketing decisions began to incorporate simple online metrics such as website visits, page views, and basic click-through rates from banner ads or email campaigns. While this marked the beginning of digital tracking, data was sparse, user behavior was hard to interpret, and personalization was virtually nonexistent. Despite its limitations, Web 1.0 laid the foundation for the more dynamic and data-rich phases that followed.
- **Web 2.0 (Interactive Web):** With the advent of Web 2.0, known as the Interactive Web, marketing underwent a major transformation driven by the rise of social media and user-generated content. Platforms like Facebook, Twitter, YouTube, and blogs enabled two-way communication between brands and consumers, generating vast amounts of real-time data. Marketers could now analyze user interactions, shares, comments,

and engagement metrics to better understand audience preferences and behavior. This era introduced more dynamic targeting, influencer marketing, and community-driven brand strategies, marking a shift from passive consumption to active participation in the digital marketing landscape.

- **Current Era:** In the current era of digital marketing, advanced technologies have revolutionized how decisions are made. Real-time tracking tools provide instant insights into consumer behavior across platforms, while AI-powered analytics uncover patterns, optimize campaigns, and personalize content at scale. Predictive modeling allows marketers to forecast trends, customer needs, and potential outcomes with greater accuracy. Additionally, omnichannel integration ensures a seamless and consistent brand experience across digital, social, mobile, and offline touchpoints. This data-driven, automated approach enables highly targeted, agile, and measurable marketing strategies like never before.

1.3 Importance of Digital Marketing Analytics

In the digital age, where every click, view, and interaction generates data, digital marketing analytics has become a cornerstone of successful marketing strategies. Its importance lies in its ability to transform vast amounts of raw data into actionable insights. Rather than relying on assumptions or outdated methods, businesses can now understand exactly how their marketing efforts are performing across different platforms, audiences, and channels. Analytics enables marketers to track customer behavior in real time, measure campaign effectiveness, identify what's working and what's not, and make timely, evidence-based decisions. It also supports better allocation of budgets by revealing which channels deliver the highest return on investment (ROI). Beyond performance tracking, digital marketing analytics empowers brands to understand customer journeys, personalize content, predict future behaviors, and foster stronger engagement. In a competitive landscape where attention is fleeting and consumer expectations are high, the ability to measure, analyze, and optimize every interaction is not just beneficial—it's essential.

- **Data-Driven Decision Making:** One of the most valuable contributions of digital marketing analytics is its ability to replace assumptions and guesswork with evidence-backed strategies. In traditional marketing, decisions were often based on intuition or historical trends, which left room for inefficiency and missed opportunities. Today, digital analytics empowers marketers to make informed choices using real-time data and measurable insights. Whether it's selecting the right channel for a campaign, optimizing ad spend, or refining target audience segments, decisions can now be grounded in actual user behavior, performance metrics, and predictive models.

Data-Driven Decision Making Process

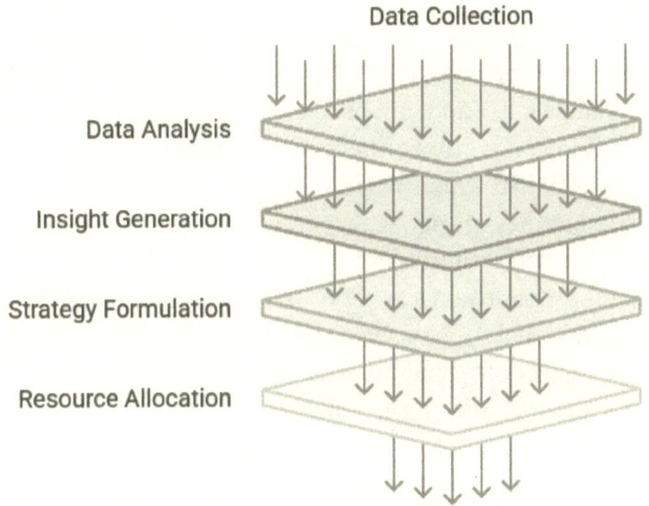

This shift toward data-driven decision-making not only improves accuracy but also increases accountability, efficiency, and confidence in strategic planning. By relying on analytics, organizations can adapt more quickly, reduce risk, and continuously optimize their marketing efforts for better results.

- **Campaign Optimization:** Digital marketing analytics plays a crucial role in optimizing campaigns by providing real-time visibility into what's working and what isn't. Through dashboards, performance metrics, and A/B testing results, marketers can quickly identify high-performing content, channels, and strategies, while also detecting underperforming elements that require adjustment. This immediate feedback loop allows teams to tweak messaging, targeting, creative assets, and budgets while a campaign is still running—maximizing impact and minimizing waste. For example, if a particular ad set is driving high engagement but low conversions, analytics tools can help pinpoint the issue, whether it's poor landing page design, misaligned messaging, or irrelevant audience targeting. This level of responsiveness ensures that marketing efforts are not just active, but adaptive—constantly evolving in response to data. Ultimately, campaign optimization driven by analytics leads to more efficient use of resources and stronger, more measurable outcomes.

- **Customer Insights:** One of the most powerful advantages of digital marketing analytics is its ability to uncover deep customer insights. By analyzing user interactions across websites, social media platforms, email campaigns, and mobile apps, marketers can gain a clear understanding of consumer behavior, preferences, and pain points. This includes tracking which pages users visit most, how long they stay, what content they engage with, and where they drop off. These insights help businesses create more personalized and relevant experiences by identifying what resonates with their audience and what turns them away. Additionally, behavioral patterns can reveal unmet needs, common objections, and barriers to conversion—enabling brands to improve product offerings, tailor messaging, and enhance customer journeys. In a marketplace where customer expectations are continually rising, the ability to truly understand your audience through data is not just a competitive advantage—it's a necessity for long-term success.

- **Improved ROI:** Digital marketing analytics plays a vital role in improving return on investment (ROI) by enabling more efficient and strategic allocation of resources. With access to detailed performance data, marketers can determine which campaigns, channels, or tactics are delivering the highest returns—and which are underperforming. This allows for smarter budgeting, ensuring that time, money, and effort are directed toward activities that generate the most value. Instead of relying on trial and error, analytics offers concrete evidence to guide decisions, reduce waste, and maximize impact. Whether it's reallocating spend from a low-converting channel to a high-performing one, or investing more in audience segments that show stronger engagement, data-driven resource management leads to measurable cost savings and better financial outcomes.

Digital Marketing Analytics Cycle

Ultimately, improved ROI isn't just about cutting costs—it's about making every marketing dollar work harder and more effectively.

• **Personalization:** In a digital environment where consumers are bombarded with messages daily, personalization has become essential for capturing attention and building meaningful connections. Digital marketing analytics enables marketers to deliver tailored experiences by understanding individual user behaviors, preferences, and engagement patterns across channels. By leveraging data such as past purchases, browsing history, location, and interaction frequency, brands can customize content, offers, and messaging to suit each customer's needs. This level of personalization goes beyond simply inserting a name in an email—it allows for dynamic website content, personalized product recommendations, targeted ads, and even individualized communication timing. As a result, users feel more seen and valued, which increases engagement, satisfaction, and loyalty. Ultimately, personalization powered by analytics enhances the customer experience while driving better marketing performance and conversion rates.

"Without data, you're just another person with an opinion." – W. Edwards Deming

1.4 Key Metrics in Digital Marketing Analytics

Understanding and tracking the right metrics is fundamental to successful digital marketing analytics. These key performance indicators (KPIs) provide a measurable way to evaluate the effectiveness of campaigns, content, and strategies across digital channels. At the core are traffic metrics, such as page views, unique visitors, and sessions, which reveal how many users are engaging with your site and how they navigate through it. Engagement metrics—including bounce rate, average session duration, click-through rate (CTR), and social shares—help assess how effectively content captures and holds attention. On the performance side, conversion metrics like conversion rate, cost per conversion, and goal completions indicate how well your efforts are turning visitors into leads or customers.

Equally important are acquisition metrics, which identify where your audience is coming from—be it organic search, paid ads, direct visits, referrals, or social media. These insights allow marketers to determine which channels are most effective and allocate resources accordingly. Additionally, email marketing metrics (such as open rate, click-to-open rate, and unsubscribe rate) and e-commerce metrics (like average order value, cart abandonment rate, and customer lifetime value) provide channel-specific insights that can inform targeted improvements. In an increasingly data-driven landscape, mastering these metrics empowers marketers to not only track progress but also continuously optimize campaigns, enhance user experiences, and achieve strategic goals.

Different channels require different metrics. Here are some of the most critical ones:

1.4.1 Website Analytics:

Website analytics form the foundation of digital marketing measurement, offering detailed insights into how users interact with a brand's online presence. These analytics track a variety of metrics that help marketers understand user behavior, content effectiveness, and site performance. Core metrics include page views, sessions, and unique visitors, which provide an overview of how much traffic a site receives and how often users return. Bounce rate indicates the percentage of visitors who leave after viewing only one page, serving as a signal for engagement quality. Average session duration and pages per session offer further context by showing how deeply users explore the site and how long they stay.

More advanced website analytics delve into user flow, identifying common navigation paths and potential drop-off points. Traffic source analysis shows where visitors are coming from—such as organic search, paid ads, social media, or referral links—enabling marketers to evaluate the performance of each channel. Additionally, tools like Google Analytics allow for goal tracking, which monitors actions like form submissions, downloads, or purchases, turning user activity into measurable outcomes. By leveraging website analytics, marketers can optimize user experience, improve site structure and content, and ultimately drive higher conversion rates and engagement levels.

- Pageviews
- Bounce Rate
- Session Duration
- Conversion Rate

1.4.2 Social Media Metrics:

Social media metrics are essential for evaluating the reach, engagement, and effectiveness of a brand's presence across platforms like Facebook, Instagram, Twitter (X), LinkedIn, and TikTok. These metrics help marketers understand how their content is performing, how audiences are interacting with it, and what drives visibility and growth. Reach and impressions measure the number of people who have seen a post and how many times it has appeared on screens, offering insight into content visibility. Engagement metrics—such as likes, comments, shares, saves, and retweets—indicate how audiences are interacting with the content, reflecting its relevance and resonance.

Beyond surface-level interactions, engagement rate provides a more nuanced view by calculating the percentage of users who engaged with a post out of those who saw it. Follower growth is another key indicator of brand popularity and organic reach over time. Additionally, click-through rate (CTR) and conversion metrics (such as link clicks or lead form completions) help determine how effectively social content drives traffic to a website or landing page. For paid social campaigns, cost-per-click (CPC) and return on ad spend (ROAS) are crucial for budget evaluation. By analyzing these metrics, marketers can fine-tune their content strategy, target the right audience, and maximize the impact of their social media efforts.

- Engagement Rate (likes, shares, comments)
- Follower Growth
- Reach and Impressions
- Sentiment Analysis

1.4.3 Email Analytics:

Email analytics play a critical role in measuring the effectiveness of email marketing campaigns and refining strategies for better engagement and conversions. Key metrics in this domain begin with the open rate, which indicates the percentage of recipients who opened the email, offering insight into the effectiveness of subject lines and timing. The click-through rate (CTR) shows how many users clicked on links within the email, reflecting content relevance and call-to-action performance. A related metric, the click-to-open rate (CTOR), compares clicks to opens, providing a deeper understanding of engagement among those who viewed the email.

Equally important are metrics that signal potential issues, such as the bounce rate, which measures undeliverable emails, and the unsubscribe rate, indicating the percentage of recipients who opted out. Monitoring these can help identify problems with list quality, message frequency, or content alignment. Advanced email platforms also track conversion rates, showing how many recipients took a desired action, such as making a purchase or filling out a form. Through A/B testing and segmentation, marketers can further optimize subject lines, sending times, and content personalization. By leveraging email analytics, businesses can improve campaign performance, nurture leads more effectively, and strengthen customer relationships through targeted, data-driven communication.

- Open Rate
- Click-Through Rate (CTR)
- Unsubscribes
- Conversion Rate

1.4.4 Paid Campaigns:

Paid campaign analytics provide vital insights into the performance of digital advertising efforts across platforms like Google Ads, Meta Ads (Facebook/Instagram), LinkedIn, and others. These campaigns are data-rich, enabling marketers to measure effectiveness with precision and adjust strategies in real time. One of the most important metrics is **click-through rate (CTR)**, which shows the percentage of users who clicked on an ad after seeing it—an indicator of ad relevance and creative appeal. **Cost-per-click (CPC)** and **cost-per-thousand impressions (CPM)** reflect the cost efficiency of driving traffic and brand visibility, respectively, helping marketers evaluate the return on their ad spend.

Another crucial metric is **conversion rate**, which measures the percentage of users who took a desired action—such as signing up, making a purchase, or downloading an asset—after clicking the ad. Coupled with **cost-per-conversion**, this helps assess campaign profitability. Additionally, **quality score** (in platforms like Google Ads) evaluates ad relevance, landing page experience, and expected CTR, impacting both performance and cost. **Impressions, reach**, and **frequency** offer context on audience exposure, ensuring campaigns are neither under- nor over-delivering. By analyzing these metrics, marketers can optimize bids, creatives, targeting, and landing pages to improve campaign ROI and overall marketing effectiveness.

- Cost per Click (CPC)
- Cost per Acquisition (CPA)
- Click-Through Rate (CTR)
- Return on Ad Spend (ROAS)

1.5 Data Sources in Digital Marketing Analytics

In digital marketing analytics, the quality and variety of data sources play a crucial role in generating meaningful insights and guiding strategic decisions. These sources can be broadly categorized into owned, earned, and paid media. Owned data comes from platforms directly managed by the business, such as websites, blogs, mobile apps, CRM systems, and email marketing platforms. This data includes user behavior, engagement metrics, and customer profiles, offering deep insights into how audiences interact with brand-owned assets. Earned data originates from external sources like social media mentions, reviews, and backlinks—essentially any organic interaction or word-of-mouth exposure. It provides a valuable view of brand perception, influence, and reach.

Paid data comes from advertising platforms like Google Ads, Meta Ads, LinkedIn Ads, and programmatic networks, delivering detailed metrics on ad performance, audience targeting, cost, and conversions. In addition to these media categories, data can also be sourced from search engines (e.g., Google Search Console), social media platforms (e.g., Facebook Insights, Twitter/X Analytics, LinkedIn Analytics), and e-commerce or sales platforms (e.g., Shopify, WooCommerce, or Salesforce). Marketers often integrate these diverse sources through analytics tools and dashboards like Google Analytics, HubSpot, or custom BI solutions to achieve a holistic view of performance. The ability to unify and interpret these varied data streams enables marketers to make data-driven decisions, personalize customer journeys, and continuously refine digital strategies.

1.5.1 Owned Media:

Owned media refers to the digital assets and channels that a brand directly controls, such as websites, mobile apps, blogs, and email marketing platforms. These channels are vital sources of first-party data, offering deep insights into audience behavior, preferences, and engagement. For example, website analytics can reveal which pages receive the most traffic, how users navigate the site, and where drop-offs occur. Similarly, email analytics provide data on open rates, click-through rates, and subscriber behavior, helping marketers fine-tune content and delivery strategies. Because the brand owns these platforms, data collection can be customized to align with specific goals—such as tracking conversions, sign-ups, or content downloads. Owned media data is not only rich and highly relevant but also privacy-compliant when collected and managed responsibly. Leveraging this data effectively allows marketers to build more personalized experiences, nurture customer relationships, and make strategic improvements to their digital ecosystem.

1.5.2 Paid Media:

Paid media encompasses data generated from advertising efforts where a brand invests to reach its target audience across digital platforms such as Google Ads, Facebook Ads, Instagram, LinkedIn, and display ad networks. This data provides precise metrics on ad performance, audience engagement, and cost efficiency. Key indicators include impressions, click-through rates (CTR), cost-per-click (CPC), conversion rates, and return on ad spend (ROAS), all of which help marketers evaluate and optimize campaign effectiveness. Platforms also offer granular demographic and behavioral data, enabling highly targeted and measurable outreach.

Additionally, paid media data can reveal which ad creatives, placements, and bidding strategies are most effective in driving results. By analyzing these insights in real time, marketers can make data-driven adjustments to maximize ROI and ensure that advertising budgets are allocated to the most impactful strategies.

1.5.3 Earned Media:

Earned media refers to the organic visibility and engagement a brand receives through user-generated actions such as mentions, reviews, reposts, and social media shares. Unlike paid or owned media, earned media is not directly controlled by the brand, making it a powerful indicator of public sentiment and brand reputation. It includes online reviews, customer testimonials, influencer shoutouts, press coverage, and organic social media engagement. Metrics from earned media help marketers understand how content and campaigns resonate with audiences, identify advocates or critics, and assess the broader reach of brand messaging beyond paid efforts. Tools like social listening platforms and sentiment analysis software are often used to monitor and measure earned media activity. Since earned media is typically driven by customer satisfaction and authenticity, it holds high trust value and can significantly amplify a brand's reach and credibility without additional spend. Effectively leveraging insights from earned media allows brands to enhance trust, build community, and adapt strategies based on real, unsolicited feedback.

1.6 Tools for Digital Marketing Analytics

A wide range of tools are available to help marketers collect, analyze, and interpret data across digital channels, making digital marketing analytics more efficient and insightful. Google Analytics remains one of the most widely used tools for tracking website performance, user behavior, traffic sources, and conversion paths. Complementary to it is Google Search Console, which provides data on search performance, keyword rankings, and indexing issues. For paid advertising, platforms like Google Ads, Meta Ads Manager (Facebook/Instagram), and LinkedIn Campaign Manager offer built-in analytics dashboards that allow for real-time performance monitoring, budget tracking, and A/B testing.

When it comes to social media, tools such as Hootsuite, Sprout Social, and Buffer help monitor engagement, track trends, and manage cross-platform analytics. Email marketing platforms like Mailchimp, HubSpot, and Campaign Monitor provide deep insights into open rates, click-throughs, list growth, and automation performance. For more advanced needs, Customer Relationship Management (CRM) systems like Salesforce and Zoho CRM, along with Business Intelligence (BI) tools like Tableau, Power BI, and Google Data Studio, allow marketers to integrate data from multiple sources, visualize key metrics, and generate custom reports. Choosing the right combination of tools depends on the business's size, goals, and digital maturity, but using these platforms strategically enables marketers to uncover insights, optimize campaigns, and drive smarter decision-making.

A variety of tools help marketers gather and interpret data:

- **Google Analytics:** Google Analytics is one of the most powerful and widely used tools for tracking and analyzing website and e-commerce performance. It provides a comprehensive view of user behavior, including how visitors arrive at a site, which pages they engage with, how long they stay, and where they drop off. For web analytics, it tracks metrics such as sessions, bounce rates, traffic sources, and conversion goals—allowing marketers to assess the effectiveness of content, SEO, and user experience. In an e-commerce context, Google Analytics (especially with Enhanced E-commerce enabled) captures data on product performance, transaction details, shopping behavior, cart abandonment, and revenue. This enables businesses to evaluate the full customer journey from discovery to purchase, identify friction points, and optimize sales funnels. With its customizable dashboards, event tracking, and real-time reporting, Google Analytics serves as a central hub for data-driven decision-making in both content and commerce strategies.
- **Google Search Console:** Google Search Console is an essential tool for monitoring and improving a website's presence in Google Search results. It provides valuable insights into SEO performance, helping marketers understand how their site is performing in organic search. Key metrics include total clicks, impressions, average click-through rate (CTR), and average position for individual keywords and pages. These insights allow users to identify high-performing content, uncover new keyword opportunities, and diagnose issues that may be hindering search visibility. Google Search Console also reports index coverage, revealing which pages are successfully indexed, which are excluded, and why—empowering marketers to ensure their content is discoverable. Additionally, it flags mobile usability issues, core web vitals, and security

problems like malware or manual penalties. By leveraging the data and alerts provided by Search Console, digital marketers and SEO professionals can make informed adjustments that enhance site performance, increase organic traffic, and align more closely with search engine algorithms.

- **Meta Business Suite:** Meta Business Suite is a centralized platform that allows marketers to manage and analyze performance across Facebook and Instagram seamlessly. It provides comprehensive insights into content reach, engagement, and audience demographics, making it an essential tool for social media management and performance tracking. Key metrics include post reach, impressions, likes, comments, shares, saves, and follower growth—helping brands understand how well their content resonates with users. The suite also offers ad performance data from Meta Ads Manager, including click-through rates (CTR), cost-per-click (CPC), and conversion metrics, enabling precise monitoring and optimization of paid campaigns.

  Marketers can use its scheduling features to plan and publish posts, respond to messages and comments from one inbox, and track performance across time periods and content types. The platform also provides audience insights, such as age, gender, location, and activity times, which are valuable for refining targeting strategies and boosting engagement. With its real-time feedback and user-friendly dashboards, Meta Business Suite supports data-driven decisions to improve both organic and paid efforts on two of the world's largest social platforms.

- **HubSpot, Mailchimp:** HubSpot and Mailchimp are two widely used platforms that blend Customer Relationship Management (CRM) with robust email marketing analytics, empowering marketers to build stronger customer relationships and optimize communication strategies. HubSpot offers an all-in-one inbound marketing platform that includes CRM, email automation, lead tracking, and performance analytics. It provides detailed insights into email opens, clicks, bounces, and engagement rates, along with behavioral tracking to see how contacts interact with your website and content. HubSpot's CRM integration allows businesses to map these interactions across the entire customer journey, helping to personalize emails, segment audiences, and nurture leads based on lifecycle stages.

  Mailchimp, while originally focused on email marketing, now includes CRM capabilities and powerful analytics features. It allows users to track open rates, click-through rates, unsubscribes, A/B test results, and conversion metrics, all in an intuitive dashboard. With advanced segmentation, automation, and personalized content features, Mailchimp helps marketers deliver relevant messages at the right time. Its reports also include audience growth and engagement trends, enabling ongoing refinement of campaign strategies. Both platforms are essential for marketers aiming to combine personalized outreach with measurable, data-driven results across email and customer interactions.

- **SEMrush, Ahrefs:** SEMrush and Ahrefs are industry-leading tools for SEO analysis, keyword tracking, and competitive research, widely used by digital marketers and SEO professionals to enhance organic visibility. Both platforms offer in-depth insights into keyword rankings, search volume, keyword difficulty, and traffic potential, enabling users to identify the most effective terms to target for content optimization and paid campaigns. SEMrush stands out for its domain vs. domain comparison, site audit tools, and PPC data, which allow marketers to evaluate competitors' strategies and uncover growth opportunities. It also features topic research, content optimization recommendations, and backlink analytics, making it a full-spectrum SEO suite.

  Ahrefs is renowned for its vast backlink database and powerful site explorer, which helps users understand their own backlink profiles and monitor competitors' link-building activities. Its Content Explorer and Rank Tracker tools provide actionable insights on which pages perform best and how keyword positions shift over time. Both platforms also offer technical SEO diagnostics, such as crawl errors, broken links, and performance issues that can affect rankings. By leveraging these tools, marketers gain a strategic edge in optimizing on-page and off-page SEO, increasing search visibility, and driving sustainable organic traffic.

- **Hootsuite, Sprout Social:** Hootsuite and Sprout Social are powerful social media management platforms that help marketers analyze performance, schedule content, and engage with audiences across multiple social networks from a single dashboard. Both tools offer robust analytics features, including metrics on reach, impressions, engagement rates, follower growth, and post performance—allowing teams to assess what content resonates best and when audiences are most active. They support integration with major platforms like Facebook, Instagram, Twitter/X, LinkedIn, and YouTube, providing a centralized view of social media efforts.

Hootsuite is particularly known for its intuitive content calendar and bulk scheduling capabilities, making it easy to plan and automate posts across channels. It also includes social listening tools that help track brand mentions, keywords, and hashtags. Sprout Social goes further with advanced audience segmentation, sentiment analysis, and team collaboration tools, making it ideal for businesses focused on social customer care. It also offers detailed reporting features with customizable templates for client or stakeholder presentations. Together, these platforms streamline social media workflows, optimize content strategies, and provide the insights needed to boost brand engagement and visibility in a data-driven way.

1.7 Challenges in Digital Marketing Analytics

Despite its transformative potential, digital marketing analytics comes with several significant challenges that marketers must navigate to fully harness its value. One of the foremost issues is data fragmentation, where information is scattered across various platforms—web analytics, CRM systems, email platforms, social media channels—making it difficult to gain a unified view of customer behavior. Data privacy and compliance, particularly with regulations like GDPR and CCPA, also pose ongoing challenges, requiring marketers to handle data transparently and ethically while still striving for personalization. Another major hurdle is the lack of analytical expertise—many organizations struggle with a skills gap in interpreting complex datasets and converting raw data into actionable insights. Additionally, real-time analysis and attribution modeling remain difficult, especially when tracking multi-channel journeys or offline conversions. There is also the persistent problem of data accuracy and quality, where errors, duplicate entries, or outdated information can skew performance measurement and lead to misguided strategies. Lastly, with the rapid evolution of digital platforms and tools, staying updated and choosing the right analytics stack can be overwhelming. Addressing these challenges requires a combination of the right technology, skilled talent, and a culture committed to data-driven decision-making.

Despite its power, analytics has limitations:

- **Data Overload:** In the age of digital transformation, marketers have access to an unprecedented volume of data—but this abundance can quickly become overwhelming. Data overload occurs when the sheer quantity of metrics, dashboards, and sources makes it difficult to extract meaningful insights or take decisive action. With information pouring in from websites, social media, email campaigns, CRMs, ad platforms, and more, teams may struggle to prioritize what matters most. This often leads to analysis paralysis, where decision-making is delayed or impaired due to overanalyzing numerous data points without a clear direction. Instead of informing strategy, excessive data can dilute focus and mask key performance indicators under layers of less relevant noise. Overcoming data overload requires a disciplined approach to analytics—defining clear objectives, selecting the right KPIs, and utilizing dashboards that highlight only the most actionable insights. By shifting from quantity to quality in data analysis, marketers can avoid being buried in information and instead drive smarter, faster decisions.

- **Attribution Complexity:** Attribution complexity is one of the most persistent challenges in digital marketing analytics, arising from the difficulty in accurately determining which marketing touchpoint—or combination of touchpoints—ultimately led to a conversion. In today's omnichannel environment, a single customer journey might include multiple interactions across email, social media, paid ads, organic search, and more before a final purchase or lead conversion occurs. Relying on simplistic models like last-click attribution can misrepresent the impact of earlier touchpoints that played a vital role in nurturing the customer. While more sophisticated models such as linear, time decay, or algorithmic attribution attempt to distribute credit more fairly across the journey, they require significant data, expertise, and often third-party tools to implement effectively. The lack of consensus on a "perfect" model means marketers frequently struggle to justify budget allocations or optimize their channel strategies with confidence. Solving attribution complexity involves adopting more advanced analytics platforms, integrating cross-channel data, and aligning measurement frameworks with the brand's unique sales cycle and user behavior.

- **Privacy Regulations:** The rise of global privacy regulations, such as the General Data Protection Regulation (GDPR) in Europe, California Consumer Privacy Act (CCPA) in the U.S., and similar laws elsewhere, has significantly transformed how marketers collect, store, and use consumer data. These regulations are designed to protect user privacy, giving individuals greater control over their personal information and requiring organizations to operate with greater transparency and accountability. For digital marketers, this means strict limitations on tracking technologies like cookies, mandatory opt-ins for data collection, and clear disclosures on how data will be used. Non-compliance can lead to hefty fines and reputational damage. These rules also complicate personalization and targeting efforts, as previously rich data sources may become anonymized, incomplete, or inaccessible. Moreover, with browser updates (like those from Apple's Safari or Google Chrome phasing out third-party cookies), the technical landscape of tracking is shifting rapidly. Navigating these legal and ethical boundaries requires marketers to prioritize first-party data, invest in consent management platforms, and adopt privacy-first analytics tools to maintain trust while still driving performance.

- **Tool Fragmentation:** Tool fragmentation is a major challenge in digital marketing analytics, referring to the difficulty of consolidating data from a diverse array of platforms and tools into a cohesive, actionable view. Marketers often rely on multiple specialized tools—such as Google Analytics for web traffic, Meta Business Suite for social media, Mailchimp for email campaigns, and CRM systems like HubSpot or Salesforce—to manage different parts of their strategy. While each tool provides valuable insights, they often operate in silos, using different data structures, metrics, and reporting formats. This lack of seamless integration makes it difficult to perform unified analysis, understand the complete customer journey, or calculate cross-channel ROI accurately. As a result, marketers may face delays, data discrepancies, and inefficiencies when stitching together reports manually. Overcoming tool fragmentation requires the use of data integration platforms, analytics hubs, or customer data platforms (CDPs) that centralize and standardize data from multiple sources. It also demands a strategic approach to selecting interoperable tools and maintaining clean, consistent data architecture across the tech stack.

1.8 The Role of Analytics in the Marketing Funnel

Analytics plays a critical role at every stage of the marketing funnel, transforming raw data into actionable insights that guide strategy, execution, and optimization. At the top of the funnel (Awareness), analytics helps measure reach, impressions, and engagement to understand how well campaigns are capturing audience attention across channels like social media, display ads, and content marketing. As prospects move to the consideration stage, marketers use analytics to track website behavior, bounce rates, time on page, and click-through rates, which indicate interest and intent. In the conversion stage, tools like Google Analytics, CRM platforms, and attribution models help identify the touchpoints that led to sales or leads, offering clarity on what's driving results. Beyond conversion, analytics supports retention and loyalty efforts by monitoring customer satisfaction, churn rates, email open/click metrics, and repeat purchase behavior. These insights enable brands to deliver more personalized experiences, fine-tune messaging, and continuously improve their funnel performance. Ultimately, integrating analytics throughout the funnel allows marketers to reduce guesswork, maximize ROI, and create a seamless, data-driven customer journey.

Analytics supports each stage of the marketing funnel:

Funnel Stage	Analytics Use Case
Awareness	Measure impressions, reach, and traffic
Interest	Track engagement, time on site, bounce rate
Consideration	Analyze click-throughs, retargeting success
Conversion	Monitor conversion rates and cost per action
Retention & Loyalty	Evaluate repeat visits, email engagement

1.9 Future Trends in Digital Marketing Analytics

The future of digital marketing analytics is rapidly evolving, driven by advancements in technology, increasing privacy concerns, and the demand for more personalized and efficient customer experiences. One of the most prominent trends is the rise of AI and machine learning, which are enabling predictive analytics, automated insights, and smarter audience segmentation. These technologies allow marketers to anticipate customer behavior, recommend content, and optimize campaigns in real-time. Another significant shift is towards privacy-first analytics, as tools and platforms adapt to stricter regulations and the phasing out of third-party cookies. This trend emphasizes the use of first-party data and consent-based tracking to build trust while still delivering value.

Customer Data Platforms (CDPs) are gaining traction as they help unify fragmented data sources into a single customer view, enhancing personalization and lifecycle marketing. Real-time analytics is also becoming essential, allowing marketers to respond instantly to customer actions and adjust campaigns dynamically. Additionally, the integration of voice, visual, and predictive search into analytics platforms is expanding the scope of data collection and insight generation. Finally, as organizations demand more accountability and agility, data democratization—empowering non-technical teams with intuitive analytics tools—is set to redefine collaboration and decision-making. These emerging trends point to a future where analytics is not just reactive, but proactively shapes strategy and innovation across the digital landscape.

- **AI and Machine Learning:** Artificial Intelligence (AI) and Machine Learning (ML) are revolutionizing digital marketing analytics by automating data analysis and enabling predictive capabilities that go far beyond traditional reporting. These technologies process vast amounts of structured and unstructured data at high speed, uncovering patterns and trends that would be impossible to detect manually. AI-powered tools can generate real-time insights, optimize ad bidding strategies, personalize content based on user behavior, and even recommend next-best actions to boost engagement or conversions. Predictive analytics, a key benefit of ML, allows marketers to forecast customer behavior—such as likelihood to purchase, churn risk, or preferred channels—enabling more proactive and targeted campaigns. Furthermore, AI chatbots, intelligent segmentation, and sentiment analysis tools are becoming integral in enhancing customer experience and operational efficiency. As these technologies evolve, they are reshaping the role of marketers, turning them into strategic decision-makers supported by intelligent, automated systems that drive precision and performance.

- **Real-Time Data Visualization:** As the digital landscape becomes more fast-paced and competitive, real-time data visualization has emerged as a crucial tool for marketers seeking to make quick, informed decisions. Modern analytics platforms now offer interactive dashboards that present live data streams from multiple sources—such as website traffic, ad performance, social media activity, and email engagement—all in one unified view. These visualizations not only make complex data more accessible but also enable immediate response to emerging trends, campaign shifts, or customer behaviors. For instance, marketers can instantly detect a spike in bounce rate, a drop in click-through rate, or a surge in traffic from a viral post, and take corrective action on the spot. Tools like Google Data Studio, Tableau, and Power BI empower teams to filter, segment, and explore data in real time, enhancing both agility and collaboration. By turning raw data into dynamic visuals, real-time dashboards shift analytics from passive reporting to active strategy, helping businesses stay ahead of the curve.

- **Unified Customer Views:** Creating a unified customer view is becoming a cornerstone of effective digital marketing analytics, as brands strive to understand their audiences holistically across multiple touchpoints. This approach involves consolidating data from various channels—websites, mobile apps, social media, email campaigns, CRM systems, and offline interactions—into a single, integrated profile for each customer. By leveraging tools like Customer Data Platforms (CDPs), marketers can overcome data silos and achieve a 360° understanding of customer behavior, preferences, and lifecycle stages. This unified perspective allows for more accurate attribution, seamless personalization, and consistent messaging across all channels. It also enables marketers to identify high-value segments, predict future behaviors, and nurture stronger relationships with their audiences. In a world where users engage across devices and platforms, unified customer views provide the clarity needed to design cohesive, data-driven experiences that resonate and convert more effectively.

- **Voice and Visual Search:** As technology evolves, voice and visual search are transforming the way users interact with digital content—demanding marketers to adapt their strategies and metrics accordingly. With the growing use of voice assistants like Alexa, Siri, and Google Assistant, users now search conversationally, using natural language rather than typed keywords. Similarly, platforms like Google Lens and Pinterest enable visual search, allowing users to search with images instead of text. These trends are reshaping SEO and search analytics by shifting focus from traditional keywords to context, intent, and image recognition. As a result, new performance indicators—such as voice query accuracy, image match relevance, and semantic search performance—are becoming essential. Marketers must optimize for these formats through structured data, conversational content, and rich visuals. Additionally, analytics tools must evolve to capture and interpret voice and image-based interactions, providing deeper insights into how users discover and engage with content in non-traditional ways. Embracing these innovations not only enhances discoverability but also positions brands at the forefront of next-generation search behavior.

- **Ethical Data Use:** In an era of increasing digital transparency and consumer awareness, ethical data use has become a foundational pillar in digital marketing analytics. While personalization remains a powerful tool to enhance user experience and drive engagement, it must be carefully balanced with respect for privacy and user consent. Brands are under growing pressure to be transparent about how they collect, store, and use data, especially in light of global regulations like GDPR, CCPA, and evolving data protection laws. Ethical data practices involve obtaining clear consent, minimizing data collection to only what is necessary, and ensuring robust data security measures. They also require marketers to avoid intrusive tracking or manipulative personalization tactics that may violate user trust. Embracing privacy-first personalization, such as using aggregated or anonymized insights and leaning on first-party data, allows brands to remain compliant while still delivering meaningful experiences. Ultimately, ethical data use fosters long-term loyalty, builds brand integrity, and aligns marketing strategies with consumer values in a rapidly changing digital landscape.

1.10 Conclusion

Digital Marketing Analytics is the cornerstone of modern marketing strategy. By turning complex data into clear insights, businesses can reach the right audience, at the right time, with the right message — and measure every step of the journey. As digital ecosystems evolve, so too must our analytical capabilities. Mastering this domain is not just optional; it's essential.

CHAPTER TWO

The Landscape of Digital Data

2.1 Introduction

Digital marketing thrives on data. Every user interaction—whether it's a website visit, a social media like, an email open, or an app download—generates a measurable signal. In today's hyper-connected world, marketers are no longer relying on assumptions or intuition; instead, they are navigating a data-rich environment where insights come from behaviors, preferences, and real-time engagement metrics. The sheer volume and variety of data available can be both empowering and overwhelming. Each action across digital channels leaves behind a trail—a digital footprint—that, when properly collected and analyzed, provides deep insights into customer journeys and campaign effectiveness.

Digital Data Landscape

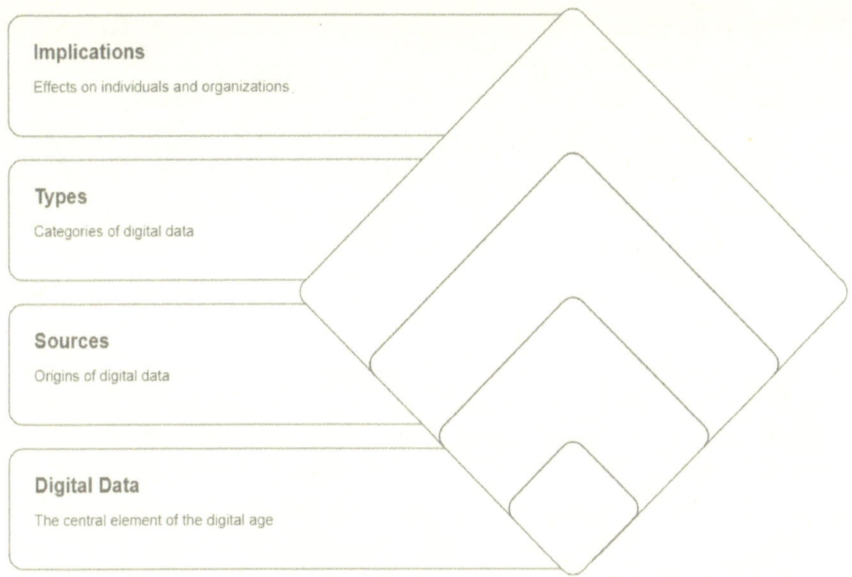

This chapter explores the diverse landscape of digital data that fuels analytics-driven marketing. It outlines the different types of data—structured vs. unstructured, first-party vs. third-party—as well as their sources, from websites and social media to CRM systems and third-party tools. Most importantly, it highlights how this data is translated into strategic action, enabling marketers to understand audiences better, deliver more personalized experiences, and measure performance with greater accuracy. Understanding the nature and value of digital data is the first step toward building smarter, more responsive marketing strategies in the digital age.

2.2 Types of Digital Data

Digital marketing relies on various types of data, each offering distinct value in shaping strategies and measuring performance. Structured data is highly organized and easily searchable—typically found in spreadsheets and databases—and includes metrics like page views, conversion rates, and customer demographics. In contrast, unstructured data consists of content that lacks a fixed format, such as social media posts, customer reviews, emails, and videos. Though harder to analyze, it provides rich insights into consumer sentiment and behavior. Bridging the gap is semi-structured data, which includes formats like JSON or XML that contain tags and markers but don't conform to strict tables—commonly seen in web tracking and marketing automation tools. Additionally, marketers work with different ownership levels of data. First-party data is collected directly from audiences via owned platforms (e.g., website analytics, email subscriptions), making it reliable and privacy-compliant. Second-party data comes from a trusted partner's first-party data, enabling mutual targeting benefits, while third-party data is purchased from external providers and used to expand audience reach—though its value is declining amid rising privacy concerns. Recognizing these data types is essential for marketers to build effective, insight-driven campaigns.

1. First-Party Data

First-party data is the most valuable and trustworthy type of digital marketing data, as it is collected directly from a brand's own audience through its owned channels. This includes information gathered from website analytics, mobile apps, email subscriptions, customer purchases, social media interactions, and CRM systems. Since the data is obtained with the user's consent, it aligns well with evolving privacy regulations such as GDPR and CCPA. First-party data offers a deep and accurate understanding of customer behavior, preferences, and lifecycle stages, enabling highly personalized marketing and more precise segmentation. For example, tracking how users navigate a website or respond to email campaigns can help refine content strategies, optimize user experiences, and improve conversion rates. Moreover, because this data comes from actual interactions with a brand, it tends to be more relevant and timely compared to second- or third-party sources. As digital privacy becomes a top concern, leveraging first-party data effectively is critical for building long-term customer trust and creating data-driven marketing strategies.

- Data collected directly from your audience.
- Examples: Website behavior, email subscriptions, CRM records.
- Value: Highly reliable and privacy-compliant.

2. Second-Party Data

Second-party data is essentially someone else's first-party data that is shared directly through a trusted partnership. It comes from a source that has collected the data directly from its own audience, such as a business partner, publisher, or platform. This data is often shared or exchanged through mutual agreements and is considered more reliable and relevant than third-party data, as it is typically collected with user consent and aligned to specific use cases. For instance, an airline might share customer travel data with a hotel chain to offer personalized vacation packages. Since second-party data originates from a known and reputable partner, marketers can use it to expand their reach, improve targeting, and uncover new audience segments without sacrificing data accuracy or privacy compliance. The value of second-party data lies in its ability to extend insights beyond a brand's own ecosystem while maintaining control, transparency, and quality assurance—making it an increasingly attractive option in the age of data privacy.

- Someone else's first-party data shared with you through partnerships.
- Examples: Data-sharing between brands or platforms.

3. Third-Party Data

Third-party data is information collected and aggregated by external organizations that do not have a direct relationship with the individuals from whom the data originates. These data providers gather insights from various sources such as websites, apps, surveys, and public records, and then sell or license this information to marketers looking to enhance audience targeting. Common uses of third-party data include audience expansion, demographic enrichment, and behavioral targeting across platforms. However, while third-party data offers scale and breadth, it often lacks the accuracy and specificity of first- or second-party sources. Moreover, growing concerns over data privacy, user consent, and regulatory compliance—particularly under laws like GDPR and CCPA—have significantly impacted its usage. Major tech platforms have also taken steps to limit third-party tracking, such as phasing out third-party cookies. As a result, marketers are increasingly cautious with third-party data, shifting their focus toward more ethical, consent-based alternatives to build trust and maintain data integrity.

- Aggregated from various sources and sold by data providers.
- Examples: Demographic profiles, purchase intent data.
- Risk: Increasingly restricted due to privacy laws (e.g., GDPR, CCPA).

2.3 Structured vs. Unstructured Data

In digital marketing analytics, understanding the distinction between structured and unstructured data is key to making the most of information gathered across channels. Structured data is organized, neatly formatted, and easily stored in relational databases or spreadsheets. It includes numerical metrics and categorical information such as click-through rates, page views, email open rates, customer names, and purchase histories. Its predictable format makes it highly suitable for quantitative analysis, reporting, and automation through tools like Google Analytics or CRM systems. On the other hand, unstructured data lacks a predefined format, making it more complex to store and analyze. This category includes content like customer reviews, social media posts, videos, audio files, and chat logs. Though unstructured data is harder to process, it offers rich qualitative insights into customer sentiment, intent, and emerging trends. Advanced technologies such as natural language processing (NLP), machine learning, and AI are often used to interpret and extract value from unstructured content. Combining both types of data enables marketers to gain a more comprehensive view of their audience—balancing hard numbers with nuanced human behavior.

Structured Data

Structured data refers to information that is highly organized and easily searchable within predefined formats, such as rows and columns in spreadsheets or relational databases. In digital marketing, this includes measurable metrics like website traffic, bounce rates, conversion rates, click-through rates (CTR), and customer demographics. Because structured data is quantitative and consistent in format, it is ideal for use in reporting tools, dashboards, and automation systems. Marketers rely on structured data for performance tracking, segmentation, and predictive modeling. Tools like Google Analytics, CRM platforms, and ad managers generate structured data that can be instantly sorted, filtered, and analyzed for trends and decision-making. Its clarity and compatibility with data analysis software make structured data the foundation of most digital marketing measurement frameworks, allowing for quick insights and data-driven optimization.

- Organized in databases, easy to analyze.
- Examples: Sales figures, click-through rates, ad impressions.

Unstructured Data

Unstructured data refers to information that lacks a predefined structure, making it more complex to store, organize, and analyze compared to structured data. In digital marketing, this type of data includes social media posts, customer reviews, emails, videos, images, blog comments, voice recordings, and even live chat transcripts. Although unstructured data doesn't fit neatly into databases or spreadsheets, it holds immense value in understanding customer emotions, opinions, and motivations. For instance, analyzing user comments on social media can reveal brand sentiment, trending topics, or unmet needs. Since this data is qualitative, marketers often rely on advanced tools such as natural language processing (NLP), sentiment analysis, and machine learning to derive meaningful insights. By tapping into unstructured data, brands can go beyond surface-level metrics and gain a deeper, more human perspective on their audience—essential for refining messaging, improving customer experiences, and staying ahead of trends.

- Free-form and harder to categorize.
- Examples: Social media posts, customer reviews, images, videos.

2.4 Key Digital Data Sources

Digital marketers draw insights from a wide range of data sources, each offering a unique perspective on customer behavior, engagement, and campaign performance. Web analytics platforms like Google Analytics track on-site user behavior, including page views, bounce rates, and conversion paths, offering foundational insights into website effectiveness. Social media platforms such as Facebook, Instagram, X (formerly Twitter), and LinkedIn provide data on likes, shares, comments, reach, and engagement, which help assess brand visibility and audience sentiment. Email marketing tools like Mailchimp or HubSpot capture open rates, click-through rates, and subscriber activity, allowing marketers to fine-tune messaging and timing. Customer Relationship Management (CRM) systems, such as Salesforce or Zoho, store valuable first-party data—like customer history, preferences, and support interactions—enabling personalized engagement. Additionally, advertising platforms like Google Ads and Meta Ads supply detailed metrics on paid campaign performance, including impressions, cost-per-click (CPC), and return on ad spend (ROAS). Marketers may also tap into third-party data providers and marketing automation tools for audience expansion and advanced targeting. By integrating data from these varied sources, marketers gain a holistic view of customer journeys and can make more informed, data-driven decisions.

Source	Data Type	Usage Example
Websites	Behavior, clicks, conversions	Optimize landing pages
Social Media	Engagement, sentiment	Brand monitoring, influencer strategy
Search Engines	Keyword data, impressions	SEO and SEM targeting
Email Platforms	Open/click rates, unsubscribes	Refine content and segmentation
Mobile Apps	Session data, in-app behavior	App experience and feature usage
E-commerce Platforms	Purchase history, cart data	Product recommendation, retargeting

2.5 Data Collection Methods

Effective digital marketing begins with robust and ethical data collection methods that capture meaningful user interactions across touchpoints. One of the most common techniques is website tracking, typically implemented through cookies, tracking pixels, and JavaScript tags, which collect data on user behavior such as page views, time spent on site, and click patterns. Form submissions, like newsletter sign-ups or contact inquiries, are another valuable source of first-party data, providing explicit user information such as names, email addresses, and preferences. Surveys and feedback forms offer direct insights into customer satisfaction and expectations, while social listening tools track brand mentions, sentiment, and trending topics across social platforms. In email marketing, tracking codes embedded in links monitor open rates, clicks, and conversions. Additionally, mobile apps use analytics SDKs to monitor user engagement, feature usage, and in-app behavior. For offline-to-online integration, methods like QR code scans, promo code usage, and point-of-sale data help tie digital interactions to physical transactions. As privacy concerns grow, marketers must ensure that all data collection adheres to legal requirements like GDPR and CCPA, with clear consent mechanisms and transparency. Choosing the right method depends on the goals, platforms, and the kind of customer insights a brand seeks to uncover.

- **Cookies & Tracking Pixels:** Cookies and tracking pixels are fundamental tools in digital marketing used to identify and monitor user actions across sessions and platforms. Cookies are small data files stored in a user's browser that remember information such as login status, preferences, and browsing history, enabling personalized experiences and retargeting efforts. Tracking pixels, on the other hand, are invisible 1x1 images embedded in emails or web pages that load when a user visits a site or opens an email. They send information back to the server, helping marketers track user behavior such as page views, email opens, conversions, and more. Together, these tools allow marketers to build detailed user profiles, measure campaign effectiveness, and deliver targeted content based on user activity over time.

- **Tags & Scripts:** Tags and scripts are snippets of code embedded in websites to collect data and integrate third-party tools, playing a crucial role in modern digital marketing. These are commonly managed through platforms like Google Tag Manager (GTM), which allows marketers to deploy and update tags without altering the core website code. Tags can track events such as form submissions, button clicks, and purchases, while scripts enable functionality like retargeting ads, analytics tracking, or heatmaps. By streamlining the implementation of tools like Google Analytics, Facebook Pixel, and conversion tracking, tags and scripts enhance flexibility, reduce reliance on developers, and improve the accuracy and depth of marketing insights.

- **Surveys & Forms:** Surveys and forms are essential tools for capturing both qualitative and quantitative input from users. They allow marketers to gather direct feedback, preferences, opinions, and demographic information that may not be visible through behavioral tracking alone. Quantitative data—such as ratings, multiple-choice responses, or scale-based answers—provides measurable insights into customer satisfaction, product interest, or market trends. Qualitative input, collected through open-ended questions, offers deeper context and sentiment, revealing the "why" behind customer behaviors. Used effectively, surveys and forms complement digital analytics by adding a human perspective, informing product development, customer experience improvements, and campaign messaging.

- **APIs:** APIs (Application Programming Interfaces) allow marketers and analytics tools to pull data directly from platforms like Facebook, Twitter, Google Ads, and many others. By connecting systems through

APIs, businesses can automate data collection, consolidate performance metrics, and gain real-time insights across multiple channels. For example, APIs enable the retrieval of ad spend, impressions, clicks, and audience demographics from Google Ads or engagement metrics from social media platforms. This seamless data flow supports dashboard creation, performance monitoring, and campaign optimization, making APIs a backbone of modern, integrated marketing ecosystems.

2.6 The Role of Data in the Customer Journey

Data plays a pivotal role at every stage of the customer journey, enabling marketers to understand, engage, and convert audiences more effectively. In the awareness stage, data helps identify which channels—such as search engines, social media, or display ads—are most effective in driving traffic and visibility. During the consideration stage, behavioral data such as time spent on site, pages visited, and content downloads offer insights into user intent and interests, helping refine targeting and messaging. In the conversion stage, transaction data, clickstream patterns, and A/B testing results reveal what drives purchases or sign-ups, enabling ongoing campaign optimization. Beyond conversion, data continues to inform the retention and loyalty stages through metrics like email engagement, customer support interactions, product usage, and repeat purchase behavior. These insights support personalization, re-engagement strategies, and customer satisfaction improvements. By mapping data to each touchpoint, marketers can create a seamless, personalized experience, anticipate customer needs, and drive long-term value. Ultimately, data transforms the customer journey from a linear path into a dynamic, insight-driven relationship.

Data tracks the consumer from first interaction to final purchase—and beyond:

- **Awareness:** Awareness is a top-of-funnel marketing objective focused on making potential customers familiar with a brand, product, or service. Key metrics for measuring awareness include ad impressions—the number of times an ad is displayed—and social reach, which represents the number of unique users who see a brand's content on social platforms. These indicators help marketers evaluate the scale and visibility of their campaigns, even if users don't immediately engage. Building awareness is crucial for driving future consideration and conversions, especially in competitive markets or during new product launches.

- **Consideration:** Consideration represents the stage where potential customers actively engage with a brand's content as they evaluate options before making a purchase decision. Key metrics at this stage include page views, which show how many times users visit product or service pages, and video watches, indicating interest in learning more through multimedia content. These behaviors signal that audiences are moving beyond mere awareness and are beginning to explore, compare, and gather information—making this a critical phase for nurturing leads and building trust.

- **Conversion:** Conversion marks the stage where a prospect takes a desired action that moves them closer to becoming a customer. Common conversion metrics include clicks on calls-to-action, purchases made through e-commerce platforms, and form submissions such as sign-ups or inquiries. Tracking conversions helps marketers measure the effectiveness of their campaigns in driving tangible results and achieving business goals, making it a key focus for optimizing marketing strategies and maximizing return on investment.

- **Loyalty:** Loyalty reflects the ongoing relationship between a brand and its customers after an initial purchase, emphasizing retention and long-term value. Key indicators of loyalty include repeat visits to the website or app, continued engagement with content or communications (like social media interactions or email opens), and customer reviews or testimonials. Fostering loyalty helps build brand advocacy, encourages repeat purchases, and creates a strong community of satisfied customers who can drive organic growth.

2.7 Data Privacy and Ethics

In the age of digital marketing, data privacy and ethics have become critical considerations that directly influence consumer trust and brand reputation. As marketers collect increasing volumes of personal and behavioral data, they must navigate complex regulations such as the **General Data Protection Regulation (GDPR),California Consumer Privacy Act (CCPA)**, and other global privacy laws that govern how data is collected, stored, and used. These laws emphasize **transparency, consent, and control**, requiring businesses to clearly inform users about data usage and give them the option to opt out. Ethically, marketers have a responsibility to prioritize user privacy by implementing secure data practices, avoiding intrusive tracking, and not exploiting sensitive information. Ethical data usage also means being honest about how data will be used—whether for personalization, remarketing, or analytics—and ensuring that it enhances user experiences rather than invades them. With growing public awareness around digital rights, companies that adopt ethical data strategies and uphold privacy standards not only comply with the law but also build deeper, trust-based relationships with their customers. In today's data-driven world, respecting privacy isn't just a legal necessity—it's a competitive advantage.

With great data comes great responsibility. Marketers must navigate:

- **Regulations:** Regulations like GDPR (General Data Protection Regulation) and CCPA (California Consumer Privacy Act) are legal frameworks designed to protect user privacy and govern how companies collect, store, and use personal data. These laws require businesses to obtain clear consent before tracking or processing data, provide transparency about data usage, and offer users rights to access, delete, or restrict their information. Compliance with such regulations is critical for marketers to avoid hefty fines, maintain customer trust, and operate ethically in an increasingly privacy-conscious digital landscape.
- **User Consent:** User consent refers to obtaining clear, informed permission from individuals before collecting, tracking, or processing their personal data. This typically involves explicit opt-ins, where users are presented with transparent information about what data will be collected, how it will be used, and their rights regarding that data. Effective consent practices ensure compliance with privacy laws like GDPR and CCPA, build trust with users, and empower individuals to control their personal information in the digital environment.
- **Transparency:** Transparency means clearly communicating to users how their data is collected, stored, and used by a company. This involves providing straightforward privacy policies, easy-to-understand notices, and clear explanations about the purpose of data collection—whether for personalization, analytics, advertising, or sharing with third parties. Transparency helps build user trust, ensures informed consent, and supports compliance with privacy regulations by making data practices open and accessible rather than hidden or confusing.
- **Data Security:** Data security involves implementing measures to protect user information from unauthorized access, misuse, or leaks. This

includes using encryption, secure servers, access controls, regular security audits, and employee training to safeguard sensitive data. Ensuring strong data security not only prevents breaches that can harm users and damage a brand's reputation but also helps companies comply with legal requirements and maintain customer trust in an increasingly digital world.

2.8 Challenges in Managing Digital Data

Managing digital data effectively is a complex task that comes with several challenges, both technical and strategic. One of the primary issues is data overload—the sheer volume of information generated across platforms can overwhelm marketers and lead to analysis paralysis. With vast amounts of structured and unstructured data flowing in from websites, social media, mobile apps, email campaigns, and CRM systems, it becomes difficult to separate valuable insights from noise. Another major challenge is data integration—merging information from various tools and sources into a single, coherent view is often hampered by platform incompatibilities and siloed systems. Data accuracy and quality are also persistent concerns; incomplete, outdated, or duplicate data can lead to flawed analyses and misguided strategies. Additionally, ensuring compliance with data privacy laws and safeguarding sensitive customer information requires robust security protocols, legal oversight, and ongoing monitoring. The shortage of skilled professionals who can clean, interpret, and act on complex data further complicates the landscape. As businesses become increasingly data-dependent, overcoming these challenges is essential to unlocking the full potential of digital marketing analytics.

- **Data Silos:** Data silos occur when information is stored in separate, disconnected systems or departments, preventing a unified, holistic view of customer data. These silos make it difficult for marketers to integrate insights across channels, leading to fragmented strategies and missed opportunities for personalization and optimization. Breaking down data silos is essential for creating seamless customer experiences and enabling data-driven decision-making across the entire marketing ecosystem.
- **Data Quality:** Data quality refers to the accuracy, completeness, and timeliness of the information marketers rely on. When data is inaccurate, outdated, or inconsistent, it undermines the effectiveness of

campaigns, leading to poor targeting, wasted budgets, and misguided decisions. Maintaining high data quality through regular cleaning, validation, and updates is crucial for ensuring reliable insights and maximizing marketing performance.

- **Integration:** Integration involves combining data from multiple platforms and sources to create a cohesive, comprehensive view of customers and campaign performance. However, this process is often complex due to differences in data formats, systems, and real-time syncing challenges. Effective integration requires robust tools and strategies to unify disparate data streams, enabling marketers to make informed, cross-channel decisions and deliver consistent customer experiences.
- **Volume and Velocity:** Volume and velocity refer to the massive amount of data generated at high speed in today's digital environment. Without proper tools and infrastructure, this sheer quantity and rapid flow of information can overwhelm businesses, making it difficult to store, process, and analyze data effectively. Managing volume and velocity requires scalable technologies like cloud computing, real-time analytics, and AI-powered solutions to extract meaningful insights quickly and keep up with fast-changing market dynamics.

2.9 Conclusion

The digital data landscape is vast, dynamic, and full of transformative potential for marketers. As consumer interactions increasingly shift online, data becomes the lifeblood of modern marketing strategy. Understanding the different types of data, their sources, and the methods of collection is essential for building accurate insights into customer behavior. Equally important is the distinction between structured and unstructured data, the challenges in integrating and managing it, and the growing necessity of adhering to privacy regulations and ethical practices. Marketers who respect these principles not only ensure compliance but also build stronger, trust-based relationships with their audiences. In a world where data is constantly evolving, staying informed, agile, and responsible is the key to unlocking smarter, more impactful digital marketing decisions.

CHAPTER THREE

Establishing a Digital Analytics Framework

3.1 Introduction

A Digital Analytics Framework serves as a strategic blueprint that bridges the gap between marketing objectives and actionable insights. In the ever-expanding digital landscape, simply collecting vast amounts of data is not enough—what matters is how that data is structured, interpreted, and applied to support business goals. A well-defined analytics framework ensures that every metric tracked is purposeful, aligned with key performance indicators (KPIs), and linked to broader organizational outcomes like customer acquisition, retention, and revenue growth. It brings clarity and consistency to data collection, making it easier to evaluate campaign effectiveness, allocate resources wisely, and make real-time adjustments. Without such a framework, analytics efforts risk becoming fragmented, reactive, and ultimately ineffective. By laying the foundation for focused, data-driven decision-making, a digital analytics framework empowers marketers to transform raw data into measurable success.

Digital Analytics Framework Pyramid

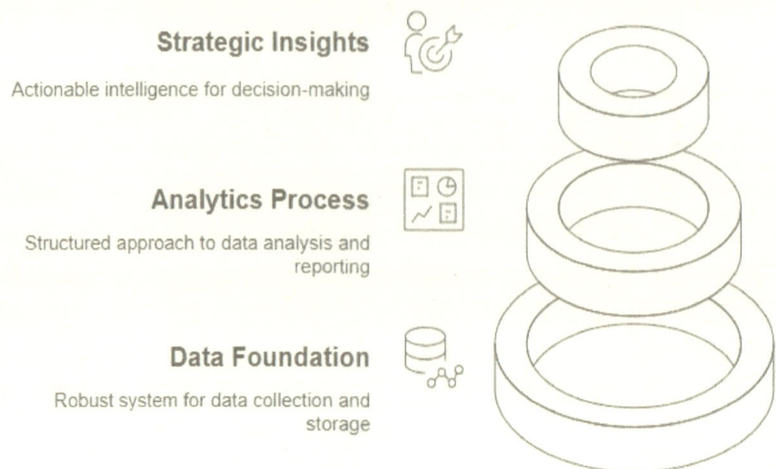

3.2 Why You Need a Framework

A Digital Analytics Framework is essential because it provides structure, clarity, and strategic direction to an otherwise overwhelming amount of marketing data. Without a framework, organizations often fall into the trap of collecting data aimlessly, resulting in confusing dashboards, conflicting metrics, and an inability to act decisively. A strong framework ensures that every data point has a purpose—it links directly to business goals, campaign objectives, or customer outcomes. It helps prioritize which KPIs to monitor, which tools to use, and how to interpret the insights in context. Moreover, a framework facilitates consistency across teams, ensuring everyone—from executives to analysts—is aligned on what success looks like and how it's measured. It also accelerates decision-making by eliminating guesswork and focusing only on relevant, actionable data. In a digital world that evolves rapidly, a framework offers the stability needed to adapt and scale analytics efforts with confidence and purpose.

- Aligns digital data with business objectives
- Focuses efforts on key performance indicators (KPIs)
- Streamlines reporting and decision-making
- Avoids "vanity metrics" and emphasizes actionable insights

3.3 Core Components of a Digital Analytics Framework

A robust Digital Analytics Framework is built on several core components that work together to ensure data is collected, interpreted, and acted upon effectively. The first component is Business Objectives, which define what the organization aims to achieve—such as increasing sales, improving customer retention, or building brand awareness. Next are the Key Performance Indicators (KPIs) that translate these objectives into measurable outcomes; for example, conversion rate, customer lifetime value, or cost per acquisition. The third component is Data Collection Methods, which include tools and technologies like web analytics platforms, CRM systems, and social media trackers to capture relevant data. Segmentation plays a vital role in breaking down data by audience type, behavior, geography, or device, allowing for deeper insight and targeted action. Another critical piece is Attribution Modeling, which helps determine how different marketing channels contribute to conversions, enabling smarter budget allocation. Finally, Reporting and Optimization involve creating dashboards, analyzing results, and continuously refining campaigns based on what the data reveals. When these components are aligned, the framework becomes a powerful system for guiding marketing strategy and delivering measurable business value.

1. Business Objectives

- Clearly define what you're trying to achieve.
- Examples: Increase sales, improve customer retention, grow brand awareness

2. Goals

- Translate business objectives into specific marketing goals.
- Examples: Drive traffic to the product page, increase newsletter sign-ups, boost mobile app installs

3. KPIs (Key Performance Indicators)

Key Performance Indicators (KPIs) are the backbone of any digital analytics framework, serving as the measurable benchmarks that reflect progress toward business and marketing goals. KPIs transform abstract objectives—such as "increase engagement" or "grow revenue"—into specific, trackable metrics that guide decision-making. For example, if the goal is lead generation, relevant KPIs might include cost per lead (CPL), lead conversion rate, or form-fill completion rate. In an e-commerce context, KPIs could include average order value, cart abandonment rate, and return on ad spend (ROAS). Social media campaigns may focus on engagement rate, click-through rate (CTR), or follower growth, while email marketing KPIs might emphasize open rates, bounce rates, and unsubscribe rates. The key is to select KPIs that are SMART—Specific, Measurable, Achievable, Relevant, and Time-bound—and that align directly with both short-term tactics and long-term strategy. Well-defined KPIs not only track performance but also uncover what's working, what's not, and where adjustments are needed to improve ROI.

- Quantitative metrics that reflect success or failure.

Objective	Goal	KPI
Increase revenue	Boost website conversions	Conversion rate, revenue per visit
Grow brand awareness	Increase content engagement	Time on site, social shares

4. Segmentation

Segmentation is a critical component of digital analytics that involves dividing your audience or data into distinct groups based on shared characteristics or behaviors. This process allows marketers to move beyond generalized insights and gain a deeper understanding of how different segments engage with content, respond to campaigns, and convert. Common segmentation criteria include demographics (age, gender, location), behavioral patterns (pages visited, time on site, purchase history), traffic sources (organic, paid, referral), and device usage (mobile vs. desktop). By applying segmentation, marketers can tailor messaging, optimize user experiences, and allocate resources more effectively. For example, knowing that returning users from email campaigns convert at a higher rate than first-time social media visitors can inform both targeting and budget allocation. Segmentation also enhances personalization strategies, enabling brands to deliver relevant content to the right people at the right time. Ultimately, effective segmentation transforms raw data into actionable intelligence, driving smarter, customer-centric decisions.

- Break down data by audience, behavior, device, channel, etc.
- Helps uncover patterns and personalize strategies.

5. Data Sources and Tools

Data Sources and Tools form the technological and informational foundation of a digital analytics framework. They define where the data comes from and how it's gathered, processed, and analyzed to generate insights. Data sources typically fall into three main categories: owned media (e.g., websites, mobile apps, email campaigns), paid media (e.g., Google Ads, Facebook Ads, influencer partnerships), and earned media (e.g., user reviews, social shares, online mentions). Each source provides unique insights into different stages of the customer journey. To harness these insights, marketers rely on a suite of analytics tools such as Google Analytics for web and traffic behavior, Google Search Console for SEO performance, Meta Business Suite for social media tracking, SEMrush and Ahrefs for keyword and competitive analysis, and email platforms like HubSpot and Mailchimp for campaign performance. Customer Relationship Management (CRM) tools also play a vital role by aggregating customer data across touchpoints. The effectiveness of a digital analytics framework depends not just on having access to data, but on choosing the right tools that integrate well, provide accurate reporting, and support real-time decision-making.

- Identify where the data will come from and how it will be collected.
- **Tools:** Google Analytics, Meta Ads Manager, CRM platforms, heatmaps
- **Methods:** Tags, UTM parameters, cookies, APIs

6. Reporting and Dashboards

Reporting and dashboards are essential for transforming raw data into clear, visual insights that drive informed decision-making. A well-designed dashboard consolidates key metrics from various data sources—such as website analytics, social media performance, email engagement, and paid campaigns—into a single, accessible interface. This allows stakeholders to monitor campaign effectiveness, track progress toward KPIs, and identify trends or issues in real time. Effective reporting goes beyond numbers; it tells a story by contextualizing data with comparisons, visualizations, and actionable takeaways. Tools like Google Data Studio, Tableau, Power BI, and Looker allow marketers to customize dashboards according to different team needs, from executives requiring high-level summaries to analysts needing detailed performance breakdowns. Automation of reports ensures consistent updates and reduces manual workload, enabling faster response times. Ultimately, reporting and dashboards are the communication link between data and action—helping teams align strategies, justify investments, and continuously optimize marketing efforts.

- Create systems for visualizing data clearly and regularly.
- **Frequency:** Daily, weekly, monthly
- **Tools:** Google Looker Studio, Tableau, Power BI

3.4 Steps to Build the Framework

Building a Digital Analytics Framework involves a strategic, step-by-step approach that ensures alignment between business goals and data-driven actions. The first step is to define clear business objectives—what are you trying to achieve through digital marketing? This could range from increasing website traffic to boosting sales or enhancing customer engagement. Once goals are established, the next step is to identify relevant KPIs that will serve as measurable indicators of success. After that, marketers must determine data sources and select the appropriate analytics tools for capturing and processing this data, ensuring that tracking is properly implemented across all digital assets. The fourth step is to segment the audience to uncover behavior patterns and personalize experiences based on user groups. Then, implement attribution models to understand how different channels and touchpoints contribute to conversions. Finally, set up reporting systems and dashboards to visualize insights, monitor performance, and continuously refine strategy. This iterative process turns raw data into a structured framework that powers smarter decisions and stronger marketing outcomes.

Step 1: Define Objectives

What is the organization trying to accomplish?

Step 2: Map Digital Goals

Break down how digital channels contribute to those objectives.

Step 3: Identify KPIs

Choose measurable, meaningful indicators (avoid vague metrics).

Step 4: Set Benchmarks and Targets

Use historical data or industry standards to establish targets.

Step 5: Select Tools and Integrations

Choose tools based on your needs, scale, and tech stack.

Step 6: Build Dashboards and Reporting Cycles

Automate where possible, and schedule reviews with stakeholders.

3.5 Example: E-commerce Analytics Framework

Step	Example
Objective	Increase online sales
Goal	Improve product page engagement
KPI	Bounce rate, cart adds, conversions
Segment	Mobile vs. desktop, new vs. returning users
Tools	Google Analytics, Shopify Reports
Dashboard Metric	Weekly revenue, top-exit pages, ROAS

3.6 Common Pitfalls to Avoid

While building a Digital Analytics Framework can drive powerful marketing outcomes, several common pitfalls can undermine its effectiveness. One of the most frequent mistakes is tracking too many metrics without clear purpose, which leads to data overload and confusion rather than clarity. Equally problematic is the lack of alignment between KPIs and business objectives, which can result in chasing vanity metrics that look good on reports but don't contribute to real growth. Another issue is inconsistent data collection, often due to poor tagging or failure to maintain tracking tools, leading to unreliable insights. Siloed data sources—where different teams or platforms don't share data—can also limit a holistic view of performance, preventing accurate attribution and campaign optimization. Additionally, ignoring data privacy regulations like GDPR or failing to secure customer data can not only damage trust but also expose businesses to legal risks. Finally, many teams falter by neglecting to act on insights, collecting data without translating it into meaningful strategies or optimizations. Avoiding these pitfalls is essential to ensure your analytics framework delivers actionable, ethical, and business-aligned intelligence.

- Tracking too many metrics without clear purpose
- Ignoring qualitative insights (like surveys or feedback)
- Not acting on data findings
- Failing to train teams on tools and frameworks

3.7 Conclusion

Establishing a digital analytics framework is a strategic investment that ensures your marketing is measurable, intentional, and impactful. It turns chaos into clarity and gives every campaign a direction. With the right framework, marketers can shift from guessing to knowing — and from reporting to optimizing.

CHAPTER FOUR

Web Analytics: Measuring Website Performance

4.1 Introduction

Your website is your most important digital asset — the virtual storefront where visitors engage, explore, and convert. But simply having a website isn't enough; understanding how it performs is what truly drives growth. This is where web analytics comes in. Web analytics is the process of collecting, measuring, and analyzing website data to evaluate user behavior, traffic sources, content effectiveness, and overall performance. It helps answer vital questions: How are users finding your site? What pages are they engaging with? Where are they dropping off? These insights enable marketers and businesses to optimize user experience, improve site design, refine content strategies, and increase conversions. In this chapter, we delve into the essential tools, key performance metrics, and strategic techniques that transform web traffic into actionable intelligence. By harnessing web analytics, organizations can make smarter decisions, ensure ROI, and build digital experiences that truly resonate with their audience.

Web Analytics Process

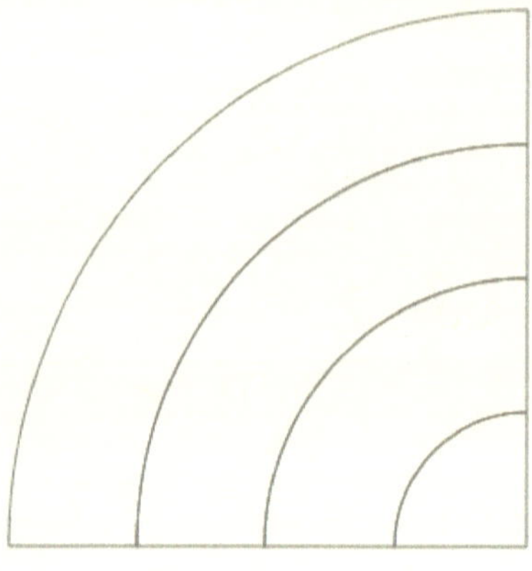

4.2 What is Web Analytics?

Web analytics is the systematic process of collecting, measuring, analyzing, and reporting data related to website activity. It provides insights into how users interact with a website—such as how they arrive, what they do while there, and where they go afterward. The goal of web analytics is to understand user behavior in order to optimize site performance, improve user experience, and drive desired actions like conversions, sign-ups, or purchases. It goes beyond simply tracking pageviews; it examines bounce rates, session durations, conversion funnels, traffic sources, device usage, and much more. By leveraging web analytics tools like Google Analytics, Hotjar, or Adobe Analytics, marketers can identify what's working, what's not, and how to enhance their strategies based on real data. In short, web analytics bridges the gap between website presence and performance, turning traffic numbers into strategic business insights.

Web analytics is the process of measuring, analyzing, and reporting on web data to understand and optimize web usage. It helps businesses:

- Track user behavior
- Identify website strengths and weaknesses
- Improve user experience (UX)
- Increase conversion rates

4.3 Key Functions of Web Analytics

Web analytics serves several essential functions that help businesses understand and enhance their digital presence. First and foremost, it enables performance monitoring, tracking how well a website meets its goals—whether those goals involve user engagement, lead generation, or sales. It also supports user behavior analysis, offering insights into how visitors navigate the site, which pages they visit, how long they stay, and where they drop off. This information is crucial for improving site design and content structure. Another key function is traffic source analysis, which identifies where visitors are coming from—such as search engines, social media, email campaigns, or direct traffic—allowing marketers to optimize acquisition channels. Web analytics also assists in conversion tracking, mapping user journeys from entry to desired actions like purchases or sign-ups. Additionally, it helps with A/B testing and optimization, allowing businesses to test variations of content or layout and identify what performs best. Overall, web analytics empowers organizations to make data-driven decisions, refine strategies, and continually improve digital effectiveness.

Measure Traffic Volume : Pageviews, sessions, and users

Measuring traffic volume is the foundation of web analytics, offering a snapshot of how much activity your website generates. Pageviews count the total number of times a page is loaded, giving insight into content popularity and engagement. However, not all pageviews are unique, as a single user can generate multiple views. Sessions refer to a group of interactions by a user within a specific timeframe—usually 30 minutes—indicating how long and how often visitors are actively engaging with the site. Users, on the other hand, represent individual visitors, whether they come once or multiple times. Tracking these three metrics together helps businesses gauge reach, repeat visits, and overall engagement trends. A steady increase in users and sessions typically reflects growing interest and visibility, while spikes in pageviews may highlight high-performing content or campaigns.

Understand Visitor Behavior : Bounce rate, session duration, pages per session

Understanding how visitors behave on your website is key to improving user experience and driving conversions. Bounce rate measures the percentage of visitors who leave your site after viewing only one page—indicating that they didn't find what they were looking for or weren't compelled to explore further. A high bounce rate could signal issues with content relevance, page load speed, or design. Session duration tracks how long a user spends on your site during a single visit. Longer sessions typically suggest that visitors are engaged and finding value in your content. Meanwhile, pages per session measures how many pages a user visits before exiting. This metric helps assess how deeply users are exploring your site and can highlight whether your navigation and internal linking strategies are effective. Together, these behavioral metrics provide powerful insights into content performance, user satisfaction, and areas needing optimization.

Track Conversions: Form fills, purchases, downloads, sign-ups

Tracking conversions is one of the most critical functions of web analytics, as it directly ties website performance to business outcomes. Conversions represent the actions you want visitors to take—whether it's filling out a form, making a purchase, downloading a resource, or signing up for a newsletter or service. Each of these actions reflects a step forward in the customer journey and provides tangible evidence of user engagement and interest. By setting up conversion goals in tools like Google Analytics, marketers can monitor how effectively different pages, campaigns, or traffic sources drive these outcomes. This data helps identify what's working and where improvements are needed, enabling optimization of landing pages, calls-to-action, and user flow. Ultimately, tracking conversions turns passive visits into measurable results, allowing businesses to refine strategies and boost ROI.

Evaluate Traffic Sources: Organic search, paid ads, social, direct, referral

Evaluating where your website traffic comes from is essential for understanding which marketing channels are driving visitors and how effective each one is. Organic search traffic comes from users who find your site through search engines like Google, reflecting the strength of your SEO efforts. Paid ads refer to traffic from advertising campaigns—such as Google Ads or social media promotions—offering insights into campaign ROI and audience targeting. Social traffic includes visits from platforms like Facebook, Instagram, LinkedIn, or Twitter, helping measure the performance of your social media strategy. Direct traffic comes from users who type your URL directly into their browser or have it bookmarked, indicating brand recognition and loyalty. Referral traffic originates from links on other websites, blogs, or directories, and can reveal valuable partnerships or content placement opportunities. By analyzing traffic sources, marketers can allocate budgets more wisely, strengthen high-performing channels, and adjust underperforming strategies to enhance overall web performance.

Optimize Content & Design

One of the most impactful applications of web analytics is in optimizing a website's content and design to improve user experience and engagement. Analytics tools reveal which pages attract the most traffic, how long visitors stay, what content they engage with, and where they drop off. This information helps identify what resonates with users and what doesn't. For instance, if a blog post has high traffic but low time-on-page, it might indicate that the content isn't meeting user expectations. Similarly, if visitors abandon a product page quickly, it may signal issues with layout, load time, or clarity of messaging. By analyzing heatmaps, scroll depth, and click patterns, marketers and designers can adjust page elements—like headlines, images, calls-to-action, and navigation—for better usability and conversion rates. In essence, data-driven content and design optimization ensures that every part of the site works in harmony to guide users toward meaningful actions.

Identify which content performs well and where users drop off

4.4 Core Metrics to Track

Tracking the right metrics is essential to evaluate website performance and guide strategic improvements. Among the most critical are engagement metrics, which reveal how users interact with your content. These include bounce rate, average session duration, and pages per session, all of which help gauge user interest and the quality of their experience. Traffic metrics like pageviews, unique users, and sessions measure the overall reach and activity on your site. Acquisition metrics—such as traffic sources (organic, paid, direct, referral, and social)—indicate where your visitors are coming from and which channels are most effective. Conversion metrics track goal completions such as form submissions, sign-ups, downloads, or purchases, directly linking site activity to business outcomes. Additionally, device and location data help you understand how and where users access your site, informing design and targeting decisions. By focusing on these core metrics, marketers can move beyond vanity stats to make data-informed decisions that enhance performance, boost engagement, and drive growth.

Metric	What It Tells You
Sessions	Number of visits to the site
Users	Unique visitors
Pageviews	Total pages viewed
Bounce Rate	% of single-page visits (no interaction)
Average Session Duration	Time spent per visit
Conversion Rate	% of visitors completing desired actions
Exit Rate	% of users who leave from a specific page
Traffic Sources	Where visitors came from (e.g., Google, Instagram)

4.5 Key Performance Indicators (KPIs)

Key Performance Indicators (KPIs) are the critical metrics that align directly with your business and marketing goals, serving as benchmarks for success. In web analytics, KPIs go beyond general data—they reflect whether your website is truly performing as intended. Common KPIs include conversion rate (the percentage of visitors who complete a desired action), cost per acquisition (CPA), customer lifetime value (CLV), and return on investment (ROI) for digital campaigns. Engagement-focused KPIs like bounce rate, average time on site, and pages per session help assess the quality of user interaction. Traffic-related KPIs such as new vs. returning visitors or channel-specific growth provide insights into acquisition effectiveness. The key to effective KPI tracking lies in choosing indicators that are specific, measurable, and relevant to your objectives. For example, an e-commerce business might prioritize purchase conversions and average order value, while a B2B company might focus on lead form completions and webinar sign-ups. By defining and monitoring the right KPIs, businesses can stay focused, measure progress accurately, and make informed decisions that drive results.

KPIs are metrics aligned to your business goals. Examples:

Goal	KPI Example
Increase lead generation	Form submission rate
Improve SEO	Organic traffic growth
Boost sales	E-commerce conversion rate
Enhance UX	Bounce rate, time on page

4.6 Popular Web Analytics Tools

Choosing the right web analytics tools is crucial for collecting accurate data, generating insights, and driving digital success. Google Analytics remains the most widely used platform, offering robust features to track user behavior, traffic sources, conversions, and audience demographics. It's ideal for both small businesses and large enterprises. Google Search Console complements it by providing insights into search performance, indexing issues, and keyword rankings. For social media performance, Meta Business Suite delivers in-depth analytics for Facebook and Instagram, while Hootsuite and Sprout Social combine social metrics with scheduling and listening capabilities. SEO specialists turn to tools like SEMrush, Ahrefs, and Moz to monitor keyword rankings, backlinks, and competitor strategies. On the email and CRM side, Mailchimp and HubSpot provide analytics for campaigns, automation, and audience engagement. Each of these tools serves a specific purpose, and when integrated, they offer a 360-degree view of digital performance—empowering marketers to make smart, data-backed decisions across all channels.

Tool	Key Features
Google Analytics 4 (GA4)	User journey tracking, events, real-time data
Hotjar / Microsoft Clarity	Heatmaps, session recordings, behavior analysis
Matomo	Privacy-focused, on-premise tracking
Adobe Analytics	Enterprise-level insights and customization

? Tip: Google Analytics 4 now focuses on event-based tracking over session-based, offering more granular insights.

4.7 Analyzing Performance by Traffic Source

Analyzing performance by traffic source allows marketers to understand which channels are most effective at attracting and converting visitors. Common sources include organic search, paid advertising, social media, referral sites, email campaigns, and direct traffic. By examining metrics such as conversion rate, bounce rate, session duration, and pages per session for each source, marketers can identify strengths and weaknesses in their digital strategy. For instance, organic traffic might show high engagement and low cost per conversion, indicating strong SEO performance, while a paid campaign may drive large volumes of traffic with a high bounce rate—suggesting a need for better targeting or landing page optimization. Segmenting performance by source also helps in budget allocation, ensuring that marketing spend is directed toward high-ROI channels. Ultimately, this level of analysis ensures that each traffic source is not only bringing in visitors but also contributing meaningfully to business goals.

Understanding how users arrive at your site helps in optimizing marketing channels:

- **Organic Search:** Organic search refers to the traffic that comes to a website naturally through unpaid search engine results. It's a key indicator of SEO (Search Engine Optimization) performance, showing how well a site ranks for relevant keywords and how effectively it attracts visitors without paid ads. Strong organic search results signal good content quality, relevance, and authority, helping drive sustainable, cost-effective traffic and long-term growth.

- **Paid Search:** Paid search refers to traffic generated through paid advertising campaigns on search engines like Google Ads. It measures the effectiveness of ads based on metrics such as clicks, impressions, cost-per-click (CPC), and conversions. Paid search allows marketers to target specific keywords and audiences, providing immediate visibility and performance data to optimize campaigns and maximize return on investment.

- **Direct:** Direct traffic refers to visitors who arrive at a website by typing the URL directly into their browser or using bookmarks. This type of traffic indicates strong brand recognition or loyal users who intentionally seek out the site, bypassing search engines or referral links. Tracking direct traffic helps marketers understand the strength of their brand presence and user engagement beyond paid or organic channels.
- **Referral:** Referral traffic consists of visitors who arrive at your website by clicking links on other websites, rather than through search engines or direct entry. These visitors come from sources like blogs, news sites, social media platforms, or partner websites. Tracking referral traffic helps marketers understand which external sites are driving interest and can inform strategies for partnerships, content marketing, and influencer collaborations.
- **Social:** Social traffic refers to visitors who come to your website by clicking links shared on social media platforms like Facebook, Instagram, Twitter, LinkedIn, or TikTok. Tracking social clicks helps marketers measure the effectiveness of their social media campaigns, understand audience engagement, and optimize content to drive more traffic and conversions from these channels.
- **Email:** Email traffic comes from users clicking links within newsletters, promotional emails, or other email campaigns. Tracking these clicks helps marketers measure the effectiveness of their email marketing efforts, understand subscriber engagement, and optimize content, timing, and targeting to boost conversions and strengthen customer relationships.

4.8 Using Funnels and Goals

Funnels and goals are foundational elements in web analytics that help visualize and measure the customer journey toward conversion. A funnel represents the step-by-step path users take on your website—such as from landing on a product page, adding an item to the cart, and completing checkout. Analyzing where users drop off in this process reveals friction points and opportunities for optimization. Goals, on the other hand, are specific actions you define as valuable—like form submissions, downloads, purchases, or time spent on a page. In tools like Google Analytics, you can set up both funnels and goals to monitor performance and identify bottlenecks. Together, they provide a powerful lens for understanding user behavior, streamlining navigation paths, and improving conversion rates.

When aligned with business objectives, funnels and goals turn raw traffic data into actionable insights that drive meaningful outcomes.

Conversion funnels map the steps a user takes to complete a desired action. Tracking funnel stages helps pinpoint:

- Where users drop off
- Which steps need improvement

Example Funnel (E-commerce):
Homepage → Product Page → Add to Cart → Checkout → Purchase

Setting up goals in analytics tools (like form submissions or video plays) allows measurement beyond pageviews.

4.9 Common Pitfalls in Web Analytics

Despite its power, web analytics can be undermined by several common pitfalls that compromise data quality and decision-making. One major issue is tracking without a clear strategy—collecting data aimlessly without aligning it to business goals leads to information overload and misinterpretation. Incorrect or incomplete tracking setup, such as missing tags or duplicate tracking codes, often results in inaccurate reports. Many teams also fall into the trap of focusing on vanity metrics like pageviews or social likes, which may look impressive but don't reflect real business impact. Another frequent mistake is ignoring segmentation—analyzing users as a single group instead of breaking them into meaningful cohorts (e.g., by source, device, or behavior) hides key insights. Additionally, neglecting context—like comparing data across irrelevant time periods or overlooking industry benchmarks—can lead to faulty conclusions. Lastly, underutilizing analytics tools or failing to act on insights turns valuable data into wasted potential. Avoiding these pitfalls ensures that web analytics becomes a reliable driver of informed, strategic action.

Mistake	Why It Matters
Tracking too many irrelevant metrics	Leads to confusion and decision fatigue
Not segmenting your audience	Overlooks critical differences in user behavior
Relying only on surface data	Lacks context or depth of user intent
Ignoring mobile performance	Most users now browse on mobile; it must be optimized

4.10 Turning Insights Into Action

Data becomes valuable only when it's translated into action. Turning insights into action means moving beyond reporting to actively improving digital performance based on what analytics reveal. For instance, if web analytics show a high bounce rate on a landing page, you might test new headlines or refine the page layout to increase engagement. If certain traffic sources drive more conversions, you can reallocate budget and focus to amplify those efforts. Regularly reviewing dashboards and performance reports should lead to A/B testing, content adjustments, refined user journeys, and even product or service enhancements. Insights should also inform broader strategies, from audience targeting to email segmentation and SEO optimization. Importantly, every action should be measured, creating a feedback loop that continually sharpens your marketing effectiveness. This is how analytics evolve from raw numbers into powerful business intelligence—fueling growth, innovation, and long-term success.

The power of web analytics lies in what you do with the data:

- **High bounce rate?** Improve content relevance or page speed
- **Low conversion rate?** Simplify checkout or improve CTAs
- **Strong blog traffic, no leads?** Add clear call-to-action buttons
- Data should inform **A/B testing, UX redesign**, and **content strategy** decisions.

4.11 Conclusion

Web analytics is the backbone of informed digital decision-making. It reveals how users interact with your website, where opportunities lie, and what obstacles stand in the way of better performance. By consistently tracking meaningful metrics, leveraging powerful analytics tools, and—most importantly—translating data into strategic actions, businesses can fine-tune every element of the digital experience. Whether the goal is to boost conversions, enhance user engagement, or optimize content, web analytics provides the roadmap. In a competitive online landscape, turning your website into a high-performing, insight-driven asset isn't just an advantage—it's a necessity.

CHAPTER FIVE

Search Analytics: SEO and SEM Insights

5.1 Introduction

Search engines are the front doors to most digital experiences. Every query represents intent, and brands that effectively appear in search results—whether through organic search (SEO) or paid advertising (SEM)—stand a better chance of connecting with their audience at the right moment. Search analytics provides the tools and data to monitor keyword performance, understand user behavior, assess campaign ROI, and uncover opportunities for greater reach. By leveraging search data, marketers can not only increase visibility but also refine messaging, improve targeting, and stay ahead of competitors. This chapter dives into the strategies and metrics behind search success, showing how to use analytics to drive smarter SEO and SEM decisions.

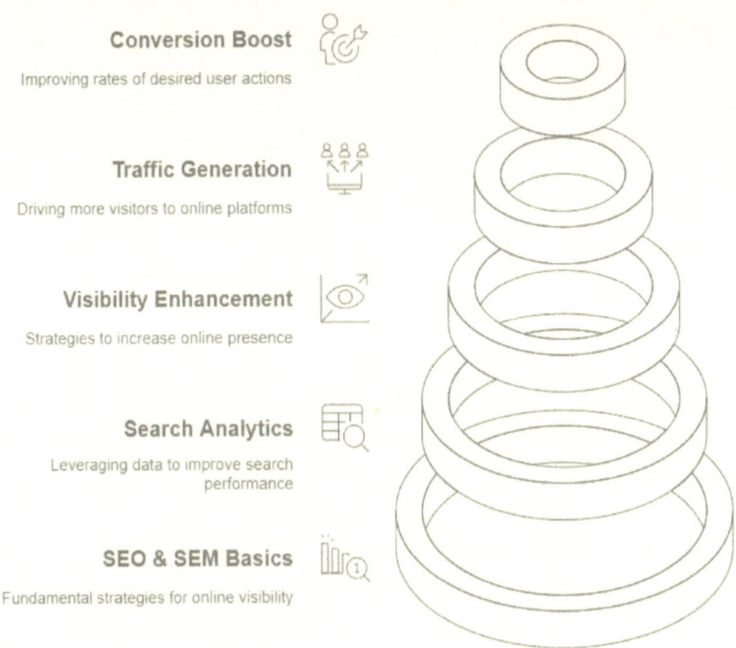

5.2 Understanding Search Analytics

Search analytics is the process of collecting, analyzing, and interpreting data related to how users discover a website through search engines. It encompasses both SEO (Search Engine Optimization) and SEM (Search Engine Marketing), offering insight into which keywords drive traffic, what content ranks well, how users interact with search listings, and how paid campaigns perform. For SEO, search analytics involves tracking organic rankings, click-through rates, impressions, backlinks, and site health. For SEM, it includes metrics like cost-per-click (CPC), quality score, ad position, and conversion rate. By understanding this data, marketers can optimize content, improve bidding strategies, target the right keywords, and boost overall search visibility. Ultimately, search analytics transforms raw keyword data into strategic insights that fuel both visibility and conversion growth.

Search analytics involves tracking, interpreting, and leveraging data from search engines to enhance visibility and performance. It covers both:

- **SEO (Search Engine Optimization):** SEO refers to the set of strategies and practices used to improve a website's visibility in organic (non-paid) search engine results. It focuses on optimizing various on-page and off-page elements to ensure that search engines can easily crawl, index, and understand the site's content. Key aspects include keyword research, quality content creation, technical SEO (such as site speed and mobile-friendliness), and backlink building from reputable sources. The goal is to rank higher on search engine results pages (SERPs) for relevant search terms, thereby increasing organic traffic. Unlike paid ads, SEO requires consistent effort over time but often results in sustainable, long-term traffic and improved brand authority. With search analytics, marketers can track rankings, click-through rates, and user behavior to continuously refine their SEO efforts.

- **SEM (Search Engine Marketing):** SEM involves using paid advertising to appear at the top of search engine results pages (SERPs), giving brands immediate visibility for targeted keywords. Unlike SEO, which builds organic traffic over time, SEM delivers faster results through platforms like Google Ads and Bing Ads. These campaigns are typically pay-per-click (PPC), meaning advertisers are charged only when a user clicks on their ad. Key components of SEM include keyword bidding, ad copy creation, landing page optimization, and ongoing performance monitoring. With the help of analytics, marketers can assess metrics such as cost-per-click (CPC), click-through rate (CTR), impression share, and conversion rate, allowing for constant refinement of budget allocation and targeting. SEM is ideal for capturing high-intent traffic and driving conversions quickly, especially when paired with a strong SEO foundation.

The goal is to evaluate **how users find your content**, which keywords drive results, and how search visibility translates into engagement or conversions.

5.3 SEO Analytics: Key Metrics

To evaluate the effectiveness of SEO efforts, marketers rely on a set of core metrics that reflect visibility, engagement, and performance in organic search. One of the most critical metrics is organic traffic, which indicates how many users arrive at the site through unpaid search results. Keyword rankings show where a site appears in search results for targeted terms, while click-through rate (CTR) reveals how often users click on the site after seeing it in the search listings. Bounce rate and session duration help assess how relevant and engaging the content is once visitors arrive. Other important metrics include backlinks (the number and quality of external sites linking to your content), page load speed, mobile usability, and crawl errors. Tools like Google Search Console and Ahrefs allow marketers to monitor these indicators and uncover optimization opportunities. Tracking these SEO metrics regularly helps marketers refine their strategies, improve content, and ultimately drive sustained organic growth.

Metric	What It Measures
Organic Traffic	Visitors coming from unpaid search results
Keyword Rankings	Position of target keywords in search results
Click-Through Rate (CTR)	% of people who clicked after seeing your result
Impressions	How often your content appeared in search
Backlinks	External links pointing to your website
Bounce Rate	% of visitors who leave without interaction
Page Speed	Load time – a critical factor for SEO and UX

? Tool tip: Use Google Search Console to monitor your site's visibility, impressions, clicks, and top-performing queries.

5.4 SEM Analytics: Key Metrics

SEM analytics focuses on measuring the performance of paid search campaigns to ensure they are cost-effective and aligned with business goals. One of the primary metrics is Click-Through Rate (CTR), which shows how compelling the ad is based on how many users click after seeing it. Cost-Per-Click (CPC) tracks how much you pay for each click, directly affecting the campaign's efficiency. Quality Score, provided by platforms like Google Ads, evaluates the relevance of your ads, keywords, and landing pages—impacting both ad rank and CPC. Conversion Rate is crucial, revealing how many clicks result in desired actions like purchases or sign-ups. Additional key metrics include Impression Share (how often your ad shows compared to competitors), Ad Position, and Return on Ad Spend

(ROAS). By continuously monitoring and optimizing these indicators, marketers can fine-tune their bidding strategies, improve ad relevance, and maximize the impact of their paid search efforts.

Metric	What It Reveals
Quality Score	Google Ads score of ad relevance and landing page
Cost-Per-Click (CPC)	Amount paid per click
Impressions & CTR	Visibility and engagement of your ad
Conversion Rate	% of visitors who completed a goal after clicking
Return on Ad Spend (ROAS)	Revenue generated per ₹ spent on ads
Ad Position	Where your ad appears on the search results page

? **Tool tip:** Use Google Ads, Bing Ads, and SEMRush to analyze SEM campaign performance.

5.5 Keyword Analysis and Intent Mapping

Keyword analysis is at the heart of both SEO and SEM strategies, as it identifies the terms and phrases users enter into search engines. However, beyond simply targeting high-volume keywords, effective marketers focus on intent mapping—understanding the why behind a search. Keywords can signal different types of intent: informational (seeking knowledge), navigational (looking for a specific site or brand), transactional (ready to make a purchase), or commercial investigation (comparing products or services). By mapping keywords to these stages of the customer journey, marketers can craft more relevant content, align landing pages, and tailor ad messaging. Tools like Google Keyword Planner, Ahrefs, and SEMrush offer insights into search volume, competition, trends, and related queries, helping refine targeting and improve performance. Intent-driven keyword analysis ensures that marketing efforts attract the right audience, improve engagement, and drive meaningful actions.

Effective search strategy starts with understanding user intent behind keywords:

Search Intent	Example Keyword	Content Type That Matches
Informational	"How to bake sourdough"	Blog posts, guides
Navigational	"Nike India site"	Brand pages
Transactional	"Buy running shoes online"	Product pages, landing pages
Commercial	"Best running shoes 2024"	Comparison pages, reviews

Tools like **Google Keyword Planner, Ahrefs,** and **Ubersuggest** help in identifying high-value keywords and tracking their performance over time.

5.6 Search Funnel and User Journey

The search funnel represents the stages a user goes through when interacting with search engines, mirroring the broader customer journey—from awareness to consideration to conversion. At the top of the funnel, users perform broad, informational searches to explore a topic or problem. As they move down the funnel, searches become more specific and intent-driven, signaling readiness to compare options or make a purchase. For example, someone might start with "how to improve sleep quality" and progress to "best memory foam mattress under ₹20,000." Understanding this journey allows marketers to align content and ads with each stage—using blog posts and guides for awareness, product comparisons for consideration, and landing pages with strong CTAs for conversion. Analyzing search behavior at each funnel stage helps refine keyword strategies, improve content targeting, and optimize ad placement, ensuring users are met with relevant experiences that guide them smoothly toward a desired action.

Search plays a vital role at each stage of the marketing funnel:

- **Top of Funnel (TOFU):** Top-of-funnel (TOFU) content is designed to attract and educate potential customers at the earliest stage of their buyer journey, primarily through SEO-focused strategies. The objective is to generate organic traffic, build brand awareness, and position your brand as a helpful resource. This content typically includes blog posts such as how-to guides, listicles, beginner's tutorials, and industry trend articles that answer common questions and address pain points. FAQs and informational landing pages optimized for long-tail and question-based keywords are also effective, often helping content appear in featured snippets on search engines. Additionally, pillar pages and topic clusters help establish topical authority by covering broad subjects with deep, interconnected content. All of this should be supported by strong SEO fundamentals, including keyword research, on-page optimization (titles, meta descriptions, headers), structured data, and internal linking. The success of TOFU content can be measured through KPIs such as organic traffic, keyword rankings, time on page, and user engagement metrics. This type of content doesn't aim to sell but rather to educate and nurture awareness, setting the stage for deeper engagement further down the funnel.

- **Middle of Funnel (MOFU):** Middle-of-funnel (MOFU) content focuses on nurturing leads who are already aware of their problems and are now evaluating potential solutions. At this stage, the goal is to build trust, demonstrate value, and move prospects closer to making a decision. Content should be more targeted and solution-oriented, highlighting how your product or service addresses specific needs. This often includes in-depth guides, comparison sheets, case studies, and webinars that provide tangible insights. Strategically placed SEM (search engine marketing) ads play a key role at this stage by targeting high-intent keywords and directing users to relevant resources such as gated content or product landing pages. Unlike TOFU content, MOFU efforts are more personalized and conversion-driven, often involving lead capture forms and calls-to-action that encourage prospects to take the next step—whether it's booking a demo, downloading a guide, or attending a webinar. Performance can be measured through metrics like click-through rates (CTR), cost-per-lead (CPL), and content downloads, all of which indicate deeper engagement and readiness to move further down the funnel.

- **Bottom of Funnel (BOFU):** Bottom-of-funnel (BOFU) content is designed to convert leads into customers by targeting users who are ready to make a purchasing decision. These prospects have already engaged with your brand and are actively comparing options or seeking confirmation before buying. BOFU strategies focus on high-intent keywords that signal readiness to act—such as "buy," "pricing," "demo," or "[product] vs [competitor]"—and drive traffic to product-focused landing pages, pricing pages, or case studies that highlight your value proposition and differentiators. Content should be clear, compelling, and conversion-optimized, featuring strong calls-to-action like "Start Free Trial" or "Request a Demo." Retargeting ads are also essential at this stage, re-engaging visitors who have shown interest but haven't yet converted by delivering personalized ads that remind them of your offering or offer limited-time incentives. Success at the BOFU stage is measured through metrics such as conversion rate, cost per acquisition (CPA), and return on ad spend (ROAS), as well as the number of demo requests or purchases. This content is all about closing the deal by eliminating friction and reinforcing trust.

Tracking the conversion path reveals how users move from search query to action, enabling optimization at every step.

5.7 Tools for Search Analytics

Search analytics tools are essential for tracking performance, uncovering opportunities, and refining SEO and SEM strategies. Google Search Console is a foundational tool for organic search, offering insights into keyword rankings, click-through rates, impressions, and indexing issues. For paid search, Google Ads provides detailed analytics on campaign performance, including CTR, CPC, conversions, and Quality Score. Tools like SEMrush and Ahrefs go further by offering competitive keyword research, backlink analysis, and domain comparisons, making them invaluable for both SEO and SEM planning. Moz is another trusted platform for tracking domain authority, keyword performance, and SERP features. For more technical audits, Screaming Frog helps identify on-site issues such as broken links, duplicate content, and crawl errors. These tools empower marketers to make data-driven decisions, optimize campaigns in real time, and stay ahead in the ever-evolving search landscape.

Tool	Use Case
Google Search Console	Organic performance, keyword tracking
Google Analytics 4	User behavior post-click
Google Ads	Paid search campaign data
SEMRush / Ahrefs	Competitive analysis, backlinks, keyword tracking
Moz	SEO audits and SERP features
Screaming Frog	Technical SEO crawling

5.8 Competitive Analysis

Competitive analysis in search marketing involves studying your rivals' SEO and SEM strategies to identify gaps, opportunities, and benchmarks for your own efforts. By analyzing competitors' keyword rankings, backlink profiles, ad copies, and landing pages, marketers can gain insights into what drives their visibility and conversions. Tools like SEMrush, Ahrefs, and SpyFu allow businesses to uncover the keywords competitors rank for organically or target through paid campaigns. You can also examine their ad spend, top-performing content, and traffic sources to understand what's working in your niche. This intelligence enables smarter keyword targeting, content creation, and bidding strategies. Regular competitive analysis not only keeps you informed but also helps differentiate your brand, refine messaging, and stay agile in response to changing market dynamics.

Search analytics is not just about your site — it's also about your **competitors.**

Questions to ask:

- Which keywords are they ranking for?
- What kind of content drives their organic traffic?
- How are their ads positioned?
- Are they targeting the same audience?

Using tools like **SEMRush, SpyFu,** or **Ahrefs,** you can uncover gaps and opportunities to outperform rivals.

5.9 Actionable Insights from Search Data

Search data isn't just for reporting — it's a powerful engine for decision-making when translated into actionable insights. By analyzing search trends, keyword performance, user behavior, and competitor strategies, marketers can uncover what content resonates, which campaigns convert, and where optimization is needed. For instance, a declining click-through rate might signal poorly written meta titles, while a spike in searches for a specific query could inspire timely content or new ad groups. High bounce rates on landing pages may indicate misaligned keyword intent or weak calls-to-action. Marketers can also segment data by device, geography, or demographics to fine-tune targeting. These insights guide tactical adjustments like re-allocating budgets, rewriting ad copy, optimizing landing pages, and prioritizing high-value keywords—ensuring search marketing efforts stay aligned with user needs and business goals.

Search analytics turns raw keyword data into smart marketing actions:

Insight	Action
High impressions, low CTR	Improve meta titles and descriptions
Strong keywords with low traffic	Optimize existing pages or create new landing pages
High bounce rate from organic	Align page content better with keyword intent
Expensive CPC but high ROAS	Increase ad budget and scale campaigns

5.10 SEO + SEM: Integrated Strategy

While SEO and SEM are often managed separately, combining them into a cohesive strategy can amplify results across the entire search landscape. SEO builds long-term organic visibility and trust, while SEM offers immediate traffic and precise targeting. Together, they create a powerful synergy—SEM data can reveal high-performing keywords that inform SEO content strategies, while SEO insights can help refine ad targeting and reduce costs. For example, a well-optimized landing page with strong SEO can improve Quality Scores in Google Ads, lowering CPCs and increasing ad effectiveness. Additionally, integrating both channels enables complete coverage of the SERP (Search Engine Results Page), increasing brand presence and reducing competition. By sharing data, aligning messaging, and coordinating campaigns across both disciplines, businesses can maximize their reach, boost efficiency, and drive better ROI from search marketing as a whole.

The most effective search strategy blends SEO and SEM:

- Use **SEM** for fast visibility and A/B testing
- Use **SEO** for long-term, cost-efficient growth
- Analyze **search terms from SEM** to guide SEO content
- Reinforce top-performing organic content with **paid boosts**

Pro Tip: Combine both in your dashboards for a unified view of your search performance.

5.11 Conclusion

Search analytics gives marketers the power to navigate and master the competitive search landscape. Whether it's optimizing content to meet the ever-evolving demands of Google's algorithm or fine-tuning paid campaigns for maximum return on investment, data is the compass that guides every decision. By leveraging keyword trends, performance metrics, and competitive intelligence, businesses can understand user intent more deeply and craft strategies that resonate. When SEO and SEM are viewed not as separate silos but as interconnected components of a unified strategy, the impact is greater reach, better targeting, and stronger outcomes. With the right insights, marketers can consistently and strategically transform search behavior into measurable business results.

CHAPTER SIX

Social Media Analytics

6.1 Introduction

Social media is where conversations, communities, and brand perceptions are built in real time. But likes and shares alone don't tell the full story. Social media analytics digs deeper to uncover patterns, measure impact, and guide smarter strategies.

In this chapter, we explore how data from platforms like Instagram, Twitter, Facebook, LinkedIn, and TikTok can be transformed into actionable business insights.

6.2 What is Social Media Analytics?

Social media analytics is the systematic process of collecting, measuring, and analyzing data from social platforms to gain meaningful insights into audience behavior, content performance, brand sentiment, and overall engagement. It goes beyond counting likes and comments—it examines how users interact with your brand, what content drives conversations, and how sentiment around your brand evolves over time. Through social analytics, marketers can assess campaign effectiveness, identify high-performing posts, monitor competitors, and spot emerging trends. By transforming raw social data into strategic intelligence, businesses can make informed decisions, refine their messaging, and strengthen their presence in an increasingly noisy and dynamic digital landscape.It helps answer questions like:

- What content works best?
- Which platform brings the most ROI?
- How are users responding to our brand?

6.3 Key Metrics in Social Media Analytics

To effectively evaluate social media performance, it's essential to track a combination of metrics that reflect reach, engagement, and impact. Reach and impressions show how far your content is spreading and how many users are seeing it. Engagement metrics—such as likes, comments, shares, and saves—indicate how audiences are interacting with your posts. Click-through rates (CTR) and conversion rates help assess whether your social efforts are driving traffic and actions on your website or landing pages. Follower growth rate reveals how quickly your audience is expanding, while engagement rate per post helps normalize interactions based on audience size. Additionally, sentiment analysis gauges the emotional tone of conversations surrounding your brand, offering insights into public perception. Tracking these metrics consistently enables marketers to understand what's working, adjust in real time, and align social media efforts with broader business objectives.

Metric	What It Tells You
Reach	How many unique users saw your content
Impressions	Total views (including multiple from the same user)
Engagement Rate	Interactions (likes, comments, shares) per follower
Click-Through Rate (CTR)	% of users who clicked a link after seeing your post
Follower Growth	Change in followers over time
Video Views / Watch Time	Attention span and video content success
Share of Voice (SOV)	Your brand's visibility compared to competitors
Sentiment Analysis	Tone and emotion in social conversations about your brand

6.4 Platform-Specific KPIs

Each social media platform has its own unique set of KPIs (Key Performance Indicators) tailored to the behaviors and formats that define user interaction on that platform. On Facebook, key KPIs include Page Likes, Post Reach, Engagement Rate, and Video Views. Instagram emphasizes metrics like Follower Growth, Story Views, Saves, and Engagement per Post. For X (formerly Twitter), important KPIs include Impressions, Retweets, Mentions, and Hashtag Performance. LinkedIn focuses more on professional engagement, so metrics like Click-Through Rate on Sponsored Content, Follower Demographics, and Post Shares are crucial. Meanwhile, TikTok centers around Watch Time, Completion Rate, and Engagement-to-View ratios. Understanding the specific KPIs that matter most on each platform helps marketers tailor their content strategy for each audience and optimize performance more effectively.

Platform	Unique KPIs
Facebook	Page likes, post reach, reactions
Instagram	Saves, story exits, profile visits
Twitter (X)	Retweets, hashtag performance, mentions
LinkedIn	Clicks from posts, follower industry/location
TikTok	Completion rate, sound performance, shares
YouTube	Watch time, subscriber gain, audience retention

6.5 Social Listening and Sentiment Analysis

Social listening and sentiment analysis are essential components of understanding how audiences truly feel about your brand, products, and industry. Social listening involves monitoring digital conversations across platforms to identify mentions, trends, and emerging issues. It helps brands stay tuned to real-time feedback, uncover unmet needs, and respond proactively to both praise and criticism. Sentiment analysis, on the other hand, uses natural language processing (NLP) to evaluate whether those mentions are positive, negative, or neutral. Together, these tools provide a pulse on brand health and public perception, allowing marketers to gauge emotional engagement and reputation. This deeper layer of insight enables businesses to craft more empathetic messaging, refine their positioning, and build stronger relationships with their communities.

Beyond metrics, social listening helps understand:

- What people are saying about your brand
- Trending topics in your industry
- Pain points or praises from your audience

Tools like Brandwatch, Sprout Social, Hootsuite, and Talkwalker can track sentiment and mentions across platforms in real time.

6.6 Content Performance Analysis

Content performance analysis helps marketers understand which types of posts are resonating with their audience and driving engagement. It involves examining metrics such as likes, shares, comments, saves, and click-through rates across different content formats—images, videos, carousels, reels, stories, and more. By identifying high-performing content, brands can replicate successful strategies and refine underperforming ones. This analysis also highlights the best times to post, preferred content themes, and tone of voice that sparks interaction. Over time, these insights inform a more strategic content calendar, improve ROI on creative assets, and ensure that every piece of content aligns with audience preferences and marketing goals.

Track performance by content type (video, carousel, image, poll) and format (reels, stories, shorts). Ask:

- Which content drives the most engagement?
- When is your audience most active?
- What hashtags or captions boost reach?

This helps optimize your posting strategy and improve ROI.

6.7 Campaign Performance Tracking

Campaign performance tracking is the process of measuring how well a specific social media initiative achieves its predefined objectives. Whether the goal is to increase brand awareness, generate leads, drive website traffic, or boost engagement, tracking the right campaign metrics is essential. These can include reach, impressions, engagement rate, conversion rate, cost per click (CPC), and return on ad spend (ROAS), depending on whether the campaign is organic or paid. By comparing these metrics against benchmarks and campaign goals, marketers can quickly assess what's working and make real-time adjustments. Campaign tracking also enables A/B testing of creatives, messaging, and targeting to refine strategies and improve outcomes. Ultimately, it ensures that social campaigns are data-driven, accountable, and optimized for impact.

Social analytics allows you to evaluate campaign-specific success:

- Engagement spikes during promotional periods
- Hashtag tracking
- Paid ad performance vs organic reach
- UTM parameters to track traffic to websites from social posts

Campaign dashboards should combine reach, engagement, conversion, and cost data for a complete picture.

6.8 Paid vs Organic Analytics

Understanding the distinction between paid and organic analytics is crucial for a balanced social media strategy. Organic analytics focus on the performance of unpaid content—measuring metrics such as likes, shares, comments, reach, and follower growth. These insights help gauge genuine audience interest and engagement, revealing what resonates without promotional support. In contrast, paid analytics track the effectiveness of sponsored posts and advertisements, emphasizing metrics like impressions, click-through rates (CTR), conversions, cost per click (CPC), and return on ad spend (ROAS). Paid data provides visibility into how targeted audiences respond to campaigns and helps justify media budgets. By analyzing both organic and paid efforts side-by-side, marketers can determine the right mix of content and investment needed to meet their goals while maximizing ROI and audience impact.

Aspect	Organic	Paid
Reach	Limited to followers and virality	Targeted reach to selected audience
Control	Less control over exposure	Full control over audience, timing
Metrics	Engagement, shares, mentions	Impressions, CTR, CPA, ROAS
Insights Use	Guide content & community strategy	Guide ad targeting & spend decisions

6.9 Social Media Analytics Tools

Social media analytics tools are essential for tracking, measuring, and optimizing performance across multiple platforms efficiently. These tools collect data in real-time and present insights through dashboards and reports, saving time and enabling data-driven decisions. Popular tools like Hootsuite and Sprout Social offer cross-platform scheduling, engagement metrics, and content analysis. Meta Business Suite provides in-depth analytics for Facebook and Instagram, including audience behavior, reach, and conversion tracking. Twitter Analytics, LinkedIn Analytics, and TikTok Insights deliver platform-specific performance data. More advanced tools like Brandwatch, Talkwalker, and BuzzSumo support sentiment analysis, influencer identification, and competitive benchmarking. By choosing the right mix of tools, businesses can streamline reporting, enhance strategy, and gain a comprehensive view of their social media impact.

Tool	Best For
Meta Insights	Facebook & Instagram analytics
Twitter/X Analytics	Tweet performance, follower growth
LinkedIn Analytics	B2B content metrics & demographic breakdown
Sprout Social	Cross-platform analytics and scheduling
Buffer	Publishing & performance tracking
Hootsuite	Campaign management and engagement tracking
Google Analytics	Tracking website traffic from social platforms

6.10 Turning Insights into Action

Collecting social media data is only half the battle—true value lies in how those insights are applied. Turning analytics into action means using metrics to guide content strategy, audience targeting, and campaign refinement. For example, if data shows that video content drives more engagement, brands can allocate more resources toward producing short-form video. If sentiment analysis reveals negative feedback around a product feature, it can prompt a quick customer service response or product improvement. Insights can also inform posting schedules, influencer collaborations, and channel prioritization. By creating a feedback loop between data and decision-making, organizations can continually evolve their social presence, enhance user experiences, and achieve measurable business goals.

Use analytics to:

- Refine your **content calendar** based on high-performing formats
- Improve **audience targeting** in paid ads
- Guide **influencer partnerships** with engagement benchmarks
- Align social goals with business KPIs (e.g., leads, sales, loyalty)

Example:

- **Insight:** Stories outperform posts on Instagram
- **Action:** Prioritize story-first content strategy with polls and swipe-ups

6.11 Challenges and Best Practices

While social media analytics offers powerful insights, it comes with its own set of challenges. Data fragmentation across multiple platforms can make it difficult to gain a unified view of performance. Changing algorithms often shift the visibility of content, complicating trend analysis. Measuring ROI remains a common hurdle, especially for organic content that doesn't directly convert. Additionally, sentiment analysis can misinterpret sarcasm or context, leading to misleading conclusions. To overcome these challenges, marketers should follow best practices: set clear, measurable goals; track a mix of quantitative and qualitative metrics; use integrated tools for centralized reporting; and regularly audit and refine their analytics strategy. Consistency in measurement and a focus on actionable insights ensure social analytics efforts remain aligned with business objectives and audience needs.

Challenge	Solution
Too much vanity data	Focus on KPIs tied to business goals
Platform algorithm changes	Stay adaptive and test content types
Measuring ROI from social	Use UTM links, custom landing pages, and conversion tracking
Fragmented data across platforms	Use integrated dashboards or analytics suites

6.12 Conclusion

Social media analytics bridges creativity and strategy. It allows brands to evolve from "posting and hoping" to posting with purpose. By listening to your audience, analyzing performance, and adjusting your approach, you can turn engagement into growth, and followers into loyal customers.

CHAPTER SEVEN

Content Marketing Measurement

7.1 Introduction

Content marketing has evolved from being a creative-driven activity to a data-powered strategy. Whether you're publishing blog posts, infographics, whitepapers, or videos, it's not enough to simply "create and distribute"—marketers must also measure performance to understand impact. Content marketing measurement allows businesses to determine what resonates with audiences, how content supports marketing goals, and where efforts should be optimized for better ROI.

Unveiling Content Marketing Measurement Strategies

7.2 The Importance of Measuring Content

Measuring content performance helps marketers move beyond assumptions. It provides concrete insights into how content is performing at each stage of the customer journey—from attracting traffic and educating prospects to converting leads and supporting sales. With clear measurement, marketers can identify which topics, formats, and channels deliver the most value and which are underperforming. This data-backed decision-making supports better content planning, budget allocation, and strategy refinement.

7.3 Content Marketing Funnel and Metrics

Content functions differently depending on its role in the marketing funnel. At the top of the funnel, blog posts and videos aim to attract attention and increase brand awareness, where metrics like traffic, bounce rate, and social shares matter most. In the middle of the funnel, lead magnets like e-books, webinars, and case studies are evaluated using metrics like time on page, downloads, and form submissions. At the bottom of the funnel, decision-focused content such as demos, testimonials, and pricing pages should be measured by conversion rates and lead quality.

7.4 Core Metrics and KPIs

There is a wide array of metrics used to evaluate content effectiveness. Pageviews and unique visitors indicate content reach, while engagement metrics such as average time on page, scroll depth, and social shares show how well content holds attention. Conversions—like form fills, sign-ups, or purchases—are critical for measuring bottom-line impact. Other indicators like backlinks and keyword rankings reflect SEO success, while customer acquisition cost (CAC) and content ROI connect marketing results to business value.

7.5 Attribution Models in Content Measurement

Since content often supports multi-touch customer journeys, using the right attribution model is crucial. First-touch attribution gives credit to the content that initiated the user's journey, while last-touch attribution credits the final piece that led to conversion. More advanced models like linear, time-decay, and position-based attribution distribute credit across different interactions, helping marketers understand how various content pieces work together to influence decisions.

7.6 Measuring Formats and Channels

Different content formats require different performance indicators. Blogs and articles are best assessed through organic traffic, backlinks, and engagement metrics. Videos require analysis of watch time, completion rates, and engagement. Downloadable assets such as guides and e-books should be tracked by lead generation rates and form completions. Each distribution channel—whether it's social media, search engines, email, or paid ads—also brings its own set of metrics, such as CTR, CPC, and referral traffic.

7.7 Dashboards and Tools

To manage content performance effectively, marketers should develop dashboards that consolidate all relevant KPIs across platforms. Tools like Google Analytics 4, Looker Studio, HubSpot, and SEMrush allow for real-time tracking and historical comparison of content performance. A good dashboard should include views by funnel stage, performance by format and topic, lead generation numbers, and conversion data, helping teams identify patterns and make strategic adjustments.

7.8 Content Scoring and Quality Assessment

While quantitative metrics are essential, qualitative evaluation plays a vital role. Content scoring frameworks allow marketers to assess the clarity, tone, relevance, and brand alignment of each piece. A simple 1–5 scale can be applied to elements like headline strength, SEO optimization, visual design, and message clarity to ensure quality remains consistent. This helps improve editorial standards and maintain trust with the audience.

7.9 Calculating ROI

Return on Investment (ROI) in content marketing can be calculated using the formula:

ROI = (Revenue Attributed to Content – Cost of Content) / Cost of Content

To improve content ROI, marketers should focus on repurposing high-performing content into multiple formats, optimizing SEO for long-term visibility, and streamlining production processes to reduce costs. Measurement ensures that time and money are spent on what truly delivers value.

7.10 Challenges and Best Practices

Content measurement comes with challenges such as fragmented data, overreliance on vanity metrics, and difficulty in tracking long sales cycles. To overcome these, marketers should prioritize business-aligned KPIs, use UTM tracking, adopt integrated tools, and conduct regular content audits. Focus should remain on meaningful metrics like conversions, leads, and customer value—not just likes or pageviews.

7.11 Conclusion

Content marketing measurement bridges the gap between creativity and performance. It empowers marketers to make informed decisions, optimize campaigns, and demonstrate the value of content initiatives. With the right metrics, tools, and analytical mindset, content marketing becomes not just an art—but a measurable, repeatable science.

CHAPTER EIGHT

Email and Mobile Marketing Analytics

8.1 Introduction

Email and mobile marketing remain two of the most direct and personalized channels in the digital marketer's toolkit. While social and search platforms dominate visibility, email and mobile provide unmatched access to users' attention—right in their inboxes or on their smartphones. To maximize their potential, marketers must track and analyze performance data to fine-tune campaigns and drive better outcomes. This chapter explores the key metrics, tools, and techniques used to measure and optimize email and mobile marketing efforts.

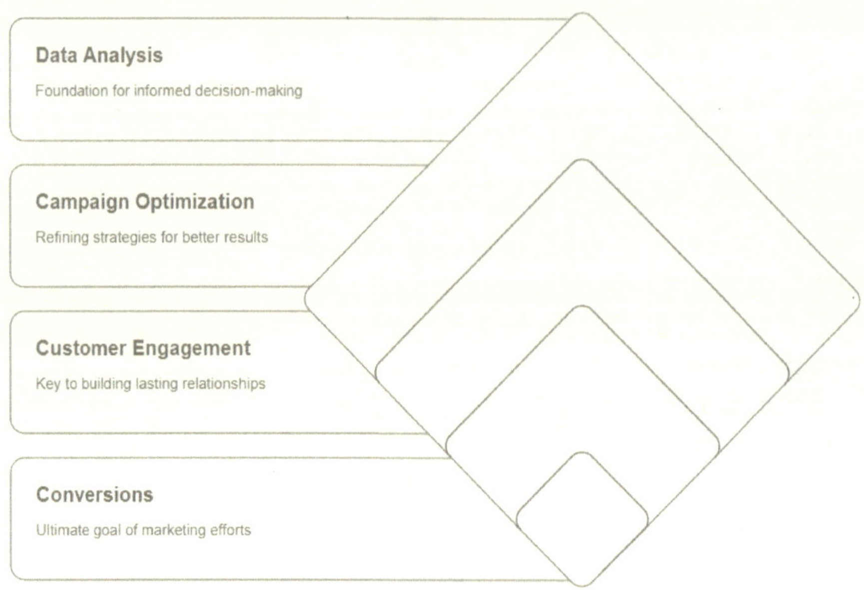

8.2 Why Analytics Matter in Email and Mobile Marketing

Unlike many digital channels, email and mobile marketing offer real-time, user-specific insights. With every campaign sent, marketers can track opens, clicks, unsubscribes, app installs, and more. This data helps in evaluating message relevance, timing, list health, and conversion impact. Analytics provide clarity on what's working, who's engaging, and how marketing efforts translate into revenue, retention, or churn.

8.3 Key Email Marketing Metrics

Email marketing analytics focuses on how subscribers interact with your messages. The most important metrics include:

- **Open Rate:** Open rate is the percentage of email recipients who open a given email. It serves as a key metric to gauge the effectiveness of subject lines, sender reputation, and the timing of the email send. A higher open rate typically indicates that the email caught the audience's attention and encourages further engagement with the content.

- **Click-Through Rate (CTR):** Click-Through Rate (CTR) is the percentage of email recipients who clicked on one or more links within the email. It reflects how engaging and relevant the email content is to the audience, indicating their interest in the offer or message. A higher CTR suggests effective messaging and call-to-action that drives users to take the next step.

- **Bounce Rate:** Bounce rate in email marketing refers to the percentage of messages that fail to reach recipients' inboxes. This can happen for two main reasons: soft bounces, which are temporary issues such as a full mailbox or a server problem, and hard bounces, which are permanent failures caused by invalid or non-existent email addresses. Monitoring bounce rates is important for maintaining a healthy email list, as high bounce rates can harm sender reputation and reduce overall deliverability. Keeping bounce rates low helps ensure that emails reach real, engaged recipients and improve the effectiveness of email campaigns.

- **Unsubscribe Rate:** The unsubscribe rate indicates the percentage of email recipients who choose to opt out of receiving future messages. This metric provides valuable insight into audience fatigue, content relevance, or the frequency of emails. A high unsubscribe rate can signal that the content isn't resonating with subscribers or that emails are being sent too often, prompting marketers to reevaluate their strategy to better engage and retain their audience.

- **Conversion Rate:** Conversion rate measures the percentage of email recipients who complete a desired action, such as signing up for a newsletter, making a purchase, or downloading a resource. This metric is crucial for evaluating the effectiveness of an email campaign in driving meaningful results and achieving business goals. A higher conversion rate indicates that the email content and call-to-action successfully motivate recipients to take the intended next step.

- **Email Sharing/Forwarding:** Email sharing or forwarding tracks how often recipients share or forward your emails to others. This metric reveals how engaging, valuable, or "share-worthy" your content is, helping to extend your reach organically beyond your initial audience. High rates of sharing can indicate strong brand advocacy and the potential for viral growth through word-of-mouth.

- **Spam Complaint Rate:** Spam complaint rate measures how often recipients mark your emails as spam or junk. A high spam complaint rate signals issues such as poor audience targeting, irrelevant or unwanted content, or sending emails too frequently. Monitoring and minimizing this rate is crucial to protect your sender reputation, maintain high deliverability, and ensure your emails continue reaching inboxes rather than being blocked or filtered out.

Analyzing these metrics over time provides feedback on content strategy, list segmentation, email frequency, and user preferences.

8.4 Mobile Marketing Analytics Overview

Mobile marketing includes channels like SMS campaigns, mobile app notifications, and in-app advertising. Each requires its own set of KPIs:

- **Delivery Rate:** Delivery rate is the percentage of emails or notifications that are successfully delivered to users' inboxes or devices out of the total sent. It measures how effectively your messages reach your audience, excluding those that bounce or fail to send. A high delivery rate is essential for ensuring that your communications have the chance to be opened and engaged with, making it a key metric for evaluating the health of your email or notification campaigns.

- **Open and Click Rates:** Open and click rates for push notifications and SMS function similarly to those in email marketing, indicating how engaged users are with your messages. The open rate shows the percentage of recipients who view the notification or message, while the click rate measures how many interact by tapping on a link or call-to-action within the message. Together, these metrics help gauge the relevance and effectiveness of your content in capturing user attention and driving desired actions on mobile devices.

- **App Downloads and Installs:** App downloads and installs are key metrics for campaigns focused on acquiring new users for mobile applications. They track how many people have successfully downloaded and installed the app, providing a direct measure of campaign effectiveness in driving app adoption. Monitoring these numbers helps marketers optimize targeting, messaging, and budget allocation to maximize user growth and engagement.

- **In-App Engagement:** In-app engagement measures how users interact with a mobile app after installation, tracking behaviors such as the number of sessions, screen views, feature usage, and retention over time. This data helps marketers and developers understand user satisfaction, identify popular or underused features, and optimize the app experience to encourage ongoing use and loyalty. High in-app engagement is often a strong indicator of app success and customer value.

- **Retention Rate:** Retention rate measures the percentage of users who return to an app after their initial installation over a specific period—such as daily, weekly, or monthly. It's a key indicator of user satisfaction and app value, showing how well the app keeps users engaged over time. High retention rates suggest that users find the app useful and enjoyable, while low rates may signal issues that need improvement to reduce churn.

- **Churn Rate:** Churn rate is the percentage of users who stop using an app or unsubscribe from messages within a given timeframe. It reflects how many customers are lost after initial acquisition and is a critical metric for understanding user dissatisfaction, engagement issues, or the effectiveness of retention strategies. Reducing churn is essential for sustaining growth and maximizing the lifetime value of users.

- **Mobile Conversions:** Mobile conversions refer to any desired actions users complete on their mobile devices as a result of a campaign, such as making purchases, signing up for newsletters, or submitting forms. Tracking mobile conversions helps marketers evaluate how effectively their mobile campaigns drive meaningful engagement and business outcomes, enabling optimization for the growing number of users interacting through smartphones and tablets.

Analytics platforms like Firebase, Mixpanel, and Adjust provide rich behavioral and event-tracking capabilities for mobile.

8.5 A/B Testing and Optimization

A/B testing plays a critical role in optimizing both email and mobile marketing. For emails, subject lines, send times, copy, and CTA placement can all be tested. In mobile, notification timing, wording, and frequency can be adjusted based on test outcomes. Testing enables data-driven decisions rather than relying on guesswork or assumptions.

8.6 Segmentation and Personalization Analytics

Understanding how different segments of your audience respond is key to effective targeting. Email and mobile platforms allow you to segment based on behavior (e.g., past purchases, inactivity), demographics, and engagement level. Measuring performance across segments reveals which messages resonate best with specific audiences and helps improve personalization efforts. Personalized content typically results in higher open rates, better CTR, and improved conversions.

8.7 Tools for Email and Mobile Analytics

Several platforms help track and manage analytics for these channels:

- **Email Tools:** Email marketing tools like Mailchimp, HubSpot, Campaign Monitor, and Klaviyo provide built-in analytics dashboards that help marketers track key metrics such as open rates, click-through rates, bounce rates, and conversions. These platforms simplify campaign management by offering real-time data, audience segmentation, A/B testing, and automation features, enabling users to optimize email performance and drive better engagement with less effort.
- **Mobile Tools:** Mobile marketing tools like Firebase, OneSignal, Braze, Mixpanel, and AppsFlyer offer powerful analytics and messaging capabilities that provide deep insights into app user behavior and campaign performance. These platforms track metrics such as user engagement, retention, in-app actions, push notification effectiveness, and attribution, enabling marketers to optimize app experiences and personalize messaging for better results across the mobile journey.
- **Unified Platforms:** Unified platforms such as Salesforce Marketing Cloud and Adobe Campaign integrate data and campaign management across multiple channels—including email, SMS, and app push notifications—into a single system. This integration enables marketers to create seamless, consistent customer experiences, coordinate messaging, and gain a holistic view of audience interactions. By breaking down channel silos, these platforms help optimize cross-channel strategies and improve overall marketing effectiveness.

These tools support real-time reporting, historical tracking, automation triggers, and funnel analysis for optimizing campaigns.

8.8 Integrating Analytics with CRM and Attribution

Email and mobile data gain more value when integrated with customer relationship management (CRM) systems and attribution models. This allows marketers to track the full lifecycle—from initial engagement to conversion and retention—providing a 360-degree view of each user. Attribution helps understand whether a conversion came from an email, push notification, or other channel, allowing smarter campaign planning and budget allocation.

8.9 Privacy and Compliance Considerations

Email and mobile marketing are governed by strict regulations such as GDPR, CAN-SPAM, and India's DPDP Act. Marketers must ensure that analytics practices respect user consent, allow easy opt-outs, and protect personal data. Transparent data collection, anonymization, and secure storage are essential to maintain compliance and user trust.

8.10 Conclusion

Email and mobile marketing analytics offer powerful insights into user behavior and campaign effectiveness. By tracking key metrics, running tests, segmenting intelligently, and integrating with broader marketing data, brands can optimize their direct communication strategies. As consumer attention becomes harder to earn, the ability to measure and refine these highly personal channels becomes a competitive advantage.

Digital Campaign Measurement and ROI

Introduction

In the digital age, running a marketing campaign is only half the equation — the other half lies in accurately measuring its effectiveness. Digital campaign measurement and ROI (Return on Investment) evaluation are critical for understanding what works, what doesn't, and how marketing efforts translate into tangible business outcomes. This chapter explores the methodologies, key performance indicators (KPIs), tools, and best practices used to measure digital campaign success and calculate ROI.

Unveiling Digital Campaign Effectiveness

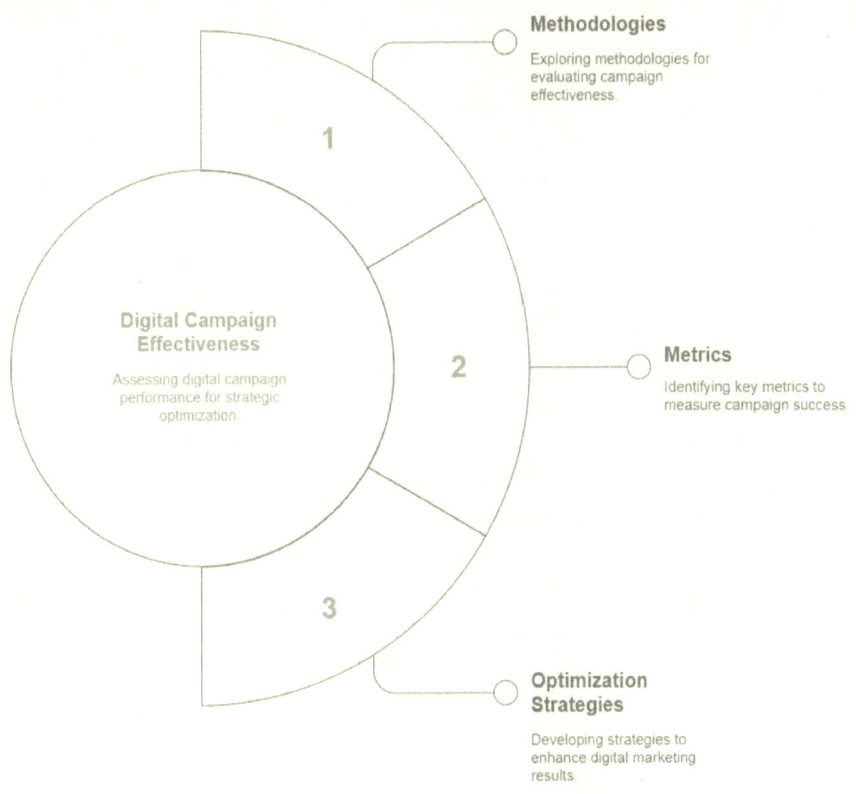

1. Importance of Measuring Digital Campaigns

Measuring digital campaigns is essential for understanding their effectiveness and ensuring that marketing efforts are delivering results. In the fast-paced digital environment, every campaign—whether it's an email blast, social media promotion, or paid ad—generates data that reveals how audiences interact with your brand. Without measurement, marketers are essentially operating in the dark, relying on assumptions rather than facts. Campaign analytics help identify what's working, what needs improvement, and where resources should be allocated for the highest impact. They also support real-time optimization, allowing adjustments on the fly to boost performance. Furthermore, measurable results provide proof of ROI, helping justify marketing budgets and strategies to stakeholders. In short, tracking digital campaign performance is the backbone of data-driven marketing success.

Measuring campaign performance is essential because it allows marketers to:

- **Assess effectiveness:** To assess the effectiveness of a marketing campaign and determine whether it met its objectives, you need to evaluate both quantitative and qualitative performance against predefined goals. Start by revisiting the campaign's original objectives—whether they were to increase brand awareness, generate leads, boost conversions, or drive sales—and identify the key performance indicators (KPIs) tied to those goals.

   For TOFU content, effectiveness is typically measured through metrics like organic traffic growth, new user sessions, time on site, bounce rate, and keyword rankings. If the objective was to increase brand visibility or attract top-of-funnel prospects, a rise in traffic and engagement would indicate success.

   For MOFU campaigns, especially those using SEM ads and downloadable guides, look at lead generation metrics such as form submissions, click-through rates (CTR), cost per lead (CPL), and engagement with gated content. The goal here is to see whether your content effectively nurtured interest and moved leads further down the funnel.

   At the BOFU stage, where the focus is on conversion, you should analyze metrics like conversion rate, demo or trial signups, cost per acquisition (CPA), and revenue attribution. Retargeting ad performance and behavior on product pages are also key indicators of success.

   Finally, qualitative feedback—such as customer testimonials, sales team input, or user surveys—can provide context to the numbers and reveal opportunities for improvement. If campaign KPIs were met or exceeded and there's a clear progression through the funnel stages, the campaign can be considered effective. If not, analyzing drop-off points or underperforming assets will inform necessary adjustments.

- **Optimize in real-time:** Optimizing a campaign in real time involves continuously monitoring performance data and making agile, data-driven adjustments to improve results while the campaign is still active.

This approach helps you maximize ROI, reduce waste, and respond quickly to what your audience is telling you through their behavior.

To do this effectively, set up real-time tracking dashboards using tools like Google Analytics, Google Ads, HubSpot, or a campaign management platform. Monitor key metrics tied to your funnel stage goals—such as CTR, bounce rate, conversion rate, cost per click (CPC), and engagement rates. If, for example, a TOFU blog post is getting high impressions but low click-throughs, optimize the meta title or description. If an SEM ad at the MOFU stage has a high CPC but low conversion, test new ad copy, targeting, or landing page variants. For BOFU retargeting ads, monitor frequency and engagement; if ad fatigue sets in, refresh creatives or adjust timing.

A/B testing (or multivariate testing) is critical during this process. Run experiments on ad creatives, headlines, CTAs, and landing pages to see what resonates best with your audience. Use heatmaps or session recording tools (like Hotjar or Crazy Egg) to understand how users interact with your pages, then tweak layout or messaging accordingly.

In short, real-time optimization means staying closely connected to performance data and treating every insight as an opportunity to improve outcomes before the campaign ends.

- **Justify spend:** Justifying marketing spend to stakeholders requires clearly demonstrating the return on investment (ROI) by connecting campaign results to business outcomes. Start by aligning the campaign goals with measurable KPIs—such as leads generated, conversions, sales revenue, or customer acquisition cost (CAC). Use attribution models to show how each touchpoint in the funnel contributed to these results, whether through organic traffic growth (TOFU), lead nurturing (MOFU), or direct conversions (BOFU).

  Present a comparison between what was spent and what was earned: calculate ROI using a simple formula—(Revenue Attributed to Campaign – Campaign Cost) / Campaign Cost. Break it down by channel or tactic (e.g., SEO content, SEM ads, retargeting) to show which areas delivered the strongest performance. Visual dashboards and performance reports can help stakeholders see improvements over time, such as lower CPL, higher conversion rates, or increased customer lifetime value (CLTV).

  Also include qualitative outcomes like increased brand awareness, improved lead quality, or stronger sales pipeline metrics—especially if the campaign had a long sales cycle or indirect impact. By tying marketing efforts to tangible business results and demonstrating cost-efficiency, you provide stakeholders with the clarity and confidence they need to see the value of their investment.

- **Improve future strategies:** Improving future marketing strategies starts with a thorough analysis of past campaign performance to identify what generated the most value. This involves not just reviewing outcomes, but understanding why certain tactics worked (or didn't). Begin by segmenting campaign data by funnel stage, channel, audience, and content type. Look for patterns in high-performing assets—such as which blog topics attracted the most qualified traffic at the TOFU stage, which SEM ads drove the lowest cost-per-lead in MOFU, or which retargeting creatives had the highest conversion rate at BOFU.

  Evaluate both quantitative KPIs (CTR, conversion rate, ROI, CAC) and qualitative signals (user feedback, sales team insights, engagement behavior). For example, if video content outperformed static ads, or if long-form guides consistently converted better than short-form assets, these are insights to double down on. Use A/B test results to refine messaging, creative direction, and audience segmentation going forward.

  Then, document these findings in a post-campaign review or playbook that outlines key lessons learned and recommendations. This helps create a data-backed foundation for future strategy, ensuring resources are invested in what delivers the most value. Ultimately, the goal is continuous improvement—learning from each campaign to build smarter, more efficient, and more impactful marketing efforts over time.

2. Setting Campaign Goals and KPIs

Before launching any digital marketing campaign, setting clear goals and defining Key Performance Indicators (KPIs) is critical for success. Goals provide direction—they establish what you want to achieve, whether it's increasing brand awareness, driving website traffic, generating leads, or boosting sales. KPIs are the measurable values that indicate how effectively those goals are being met. For example, if the goal is lead generation, relevant KPIs might include cost per lead, form submissions, or conversion rate. Setting SMART goals—Specific, Measurable, Achievable, Relevant, and Time-bound—ensures that campaign performance can be tracked and evaluated objectively. Well-defined KPIs not only guide campaign execution but also enable marketers to analyze results, make informed decisions, and demonstrate value to stakeholders.

Every measurement strategy starts with clear goal-setting. Goals can be:

- **Awareness-driven:** Awareness-driven marketing focuses on maximizing visibility and recognition among target audiences, especially at the top of the funnel. The main goal isn't immediate conversion but rather to increase reach, generate impressions, and create a measurable brand lift—all indicators that more people are becoming familiar with your brand.

  Reach refers to the total number of unique users who have seen your content or ad, helping you understand how broadly your message is being distributed. Impressions measure how often your content is displayed, regardless of clicks or engagement, which is useful for understanding frequency and potential exposure. To gauge brand lift, use metrics such as branded search volume, social mentions, direct traffic increases, or brand recall surveys. Some ad platforms (like Google and Meta) also offer brand lift studies that assess changes in perception or awareness after campaign exposure.

  Success in awareness campaigns isn't always about clicks—it's about visibility, perception, and staying top of mind. Strong creative, consistent messaging, and targeting the right audiences are key. Over time, increased awareness contributes to stronger performance down the funnel, as prospects are more likely to trust and engage with brands they recognize.

- **Engagement-driven:** Engagement-driven marketing focuses on encouraging meaningful interactions with your content, signaling that your audience is not just seeing your brand—but actively responding to it. The key metrics here include click-through rates (CTR), likes, shares, comments, and other platform-specific interactions (such as saves, retweets, or video views). These metrics help you understand how compelling your messaging, creative, and value proposition are to your audience.

  CTR indicates how effective your content is at driving users to take action, such as visiting a landing page or downloading a resource. High CTR typically reflects strong messaging alignment and relevance. Likes and reactions show passive approval, while shares are more powerful indicators of advocacy—users find the content valuable enough to distribute it to their own network. Comments offer deeper insights into sentiment and engagement quality, often sparking conversations and community interaction.

To optimize for engagement, focus on producing content that is visually appealing, emotionally resonant, and relevant to your audience's needs. Use strong hooks, clear calls-to-action, and interactive elements like polls, quizzes, or questions. Monitor these metrics closely across platforms to identify what type of content and formats drive the most interaction—and refine future campaigns accordingly. High engagement often leads to increased organic reach and builds stronger relationships, making it a valuable middle step between awareness and conversion.

- **Conversion-driven:** Conversion-driven marketing zeroes in on turning interested prospects into actual customers or users by prompting specific actions like generating leads, driving sales, encouraging app downloads, or securing signups. The core metrics here track these tangible outcomes—such as the number of form submissions, completed purchases, trial activations, or account creations—which directly impact business revenue and growth.

  To succeed at this stage, campaigns focus on clear, persuasive calls-to-action (CTAs) and seamless user experiences that reduce friction. Content and ads are highly targeted, often personalized, and emphasize the product's value, benefits, and urgency—like limited-time offers or demos. Conversion tracking tools (such as Google Analytics goals, Facebook Pixel, or CRM integrations) provide insights into which channels, creatives, or audience segments deliver the best return.

  By closely analyzing conversion metrics—like conversion rate, cost per acquisition (CPA), and revenue generated—marketers can optimize budget allocation and messaging for maximum impact. Ultimately, conversion-driven efforts close the loop of the marketing funnel, turning awareness and engagement into measurable business results.

KPIs (Key Performance Indicators) must align with these goals. Some examples:

- Cost Per Click (CPC)
- Click-Through Rate (CTR)
- Conversion Rate
- Customer Acquisition Cost (CAC)
- Lifetime Value (LTV)
- Return on Ad Spend (ROAS)

3. Tools for Campaign Tracking and Analytics

To effectively measure the performance of digital campaigns, marketers rely on a variety of tracking and analytics tools. These platforms collect, organize, and interpret data, transforming raw numbers into actionable insights. Google Analytics is one of the most widely used tools, offering detailed information about user behavior, traffic sources, and conversions. Google Ads and Meta Ads Manager provide robust tracking for paid campaigns across search engines and social media platforms. Email marketing platforms like Mailchimp and HubSpot come with built-in analytics for open rates, click-through rates, and engagement. For multi-channel performance, tools like Tableau, Google Looker Studio, or Klipfolio can create dashboards that aggregate data in real-time. Tag management systems like Google Tag Manager also streamline the setup of tracking codes without needing developer input. Choosing the right mix of tools ensures that every stage of the campaign is monitored, measured, and ready for optimization.

Various digital tools assist in tracking campaign performance across platforms:

- **Google Analytics:** Google Analytics is a powerful tool for understanding how visitors find and interact with your website, helping you measure and optimize your marketing efforts. It provides insights into traffic sources, showing where your visitors come from—whether organic search, paid ads, social media, direct visits, or referrals—so you can identify which channels are driving the most traffic and conversions. The behavior flow report visualizes the path users take through your site, highlighting common navigation routes, drop-off points, and content that keeps users engaged, which is invaluable for improving site structure and user experience. Additionally, goal completions track specific actions you've defined as valuable, such as form submissions, purchases, newsletter signups, or downloads, allowing you to measure how effectively your site meets business objectives. By analyzing these key areas, Google Analytics helps you make informed, data-driven decisions to enhance your campaigns, increase engagement, and boost conversions.

- **Meta (Facebook) Ads Manager:** Meta (Facebook) Ads Manager is a robust platform that provides detailed insights into the performance of your ad campaigns across Facebook, Instagram, and other Meta properties. It offers granular data on ad insights, including metrics like impressions, reach, click-through rates (CTR), cost per click (CPC), and conversions, helping you understand how well your ads are performing in real time. The platform also breaks down demographics of your audience—such as age, gender, location, and device—allowing you to see who is engaging with your ads and tailor targeting strategies accordingly. Additionally, Ads Manager tracks actions users take after seeing or interacting with your ads, such as page likes, website visits, purchases, or app installs, enabling you to measure the direct impact of your campaigns on business goals. These insights empower marketers to optimize ad creative, budgets, and targeting to maximize return on investment and drive more effective advertising outcomes.

- **LinkedIn Campaign Manager, Twitter Analytics, etc.:** Each social advertising platform offers unique analytics tools with platform-specific metrics that help marketers understand campaign performance and audience behavior in context. For example, LinkedIn Campaign Manager provides insights tailored to a professional audience, including metrics like engagement rate, lead generation form submissions, job titles and company industries of users interacting with your ads, as well as conversion tracking for B2B-focused campaigns. This helps businesses refine targeting based on professional demographics and measure how well their content resonates with decision-makers.

  Similarly, Twitter Analytics offers data on tweet impressions, engagements (clicks, retweets, replies, likes), and followers' demographics. Twitter's real-time conversational nature means you can track trending topics and hashtag performance, understand audience sentiment, and assess the impact of promoted tweets or campaigns in driving conversations and awareness.

  Other platforms like TikTok Ads Manager, Pinterest Analytics, or Snapchat Ads provide comparable dashboards with metrics tailored to their unique user behaviors and ad formats. Leveraging these platform-specific metrics ensures campaigns are optimized for the nuances of each channel, enabling more precise targeting, messaging, and measurement aligned with your marketing objectives.

- **UTM Parameters:** UTM parameters are custom tags added to the end of URLs that allow marketers to track the source, medium, campaign, and other details of traffic coming to their website. By appending UTM parameters to links used in emails, social posts, ads, or other marketing channels, you can see exactly where your visitors are coming from and how specific campaigns perform in analytics tools like Google Analytics. For example, a URL might include tags like *utm_source=facebook&utm_medium=paid_social&utm_campaign=spring_sale* to identify traffic from a Facebook paid campaign promoting a spring sale. This granular tracking helps attribute conversions and user behavior to the right marketing efforts, enabling better measurement of ROI and more informed decisions about where to invest budget and optimize campaigns. Using consistent UTM tagging conventions is key to maintaining clean, actionable data across all your marketing channels.

- **CRM and Marketing Automation:** CRM and marketing automation systems play a crucial role in tracking and managing the entire customer journey—from lead capture to sale—by integrating data across marketing and sales activities. A CRM (Customer Relationship Management) platform records detailed information about each lead, including their lead source (where they originated, such as a specific campaign or channel), enabling marketers and sales teams to understand which efforts generate the most qualified prospects. Marketing automation tools help manage the nurturing journey by delivering targeted, timely content and communications based on user behavior and engagement, guiding leads through the funnel with personalized emails, workflows, and triggers. Together, these systems provide sales attribution by linking marketing touchpoints to closed deals, allowing businesses to identify which campaigns and interactions contributed to revenue. This holistic view empowers more effective lead management, optimized marketing spend, and improved collaboration between marketing and sales teams.

4. Attribution Models

Attribution models play a critical role in understanding which touchpoints in the customer journey contribute most to conversions. In today's multi-channel digital landscape, users often interact with a brand several times—through ads, emails, social media, and organic search—before making a purchase or completing a goal. Attribution models assign credit to these touchpoints in different ways. First-touch attribution gives all the credit to the initial interaction, while last-touch attribution credits the final one. More advanced models like linear attribution distribute credit evenly across all touchpoints, and time decay models give more weight to recent interactions. Data-driven attribution, powered by machine learning, dynamically analyzes the actual paths users take and assigns credit based on statistical impact. Choosing the right attribution model is essential for accurate measurement and informed budget allocation, helping marketers understand what's truly driving results.

Understanding which touchpoint contributed to the conversion is critical. Attribution models help allocate credit:

- **First-click Attribution:** First-click attribution gives full credit for a conversion to the very first touchpoint or interaction a customer had with your brand. This model assumes that the initial engagement—whether it's clicking on an ad, visiting a website, or opening an email—is the most influential step in starting the buyer's journey. It's useful for understanding which marketing channels or campaigns are most effective at generating initial awareness or interest. However, it doesn't account for subsequent interactions that may have played a significant role in nurturing and closing the sale, so it provides a limited view of overall performance. First-click attribution is often paired with other models to get a more balanced understanding of marketing impact across the entire customer journey.

- **Last-click Attribution:** Last-click attribution gives full credit for a conversion to the final touchpoint or interaction a customer had before completing the desired action, such as making a purchase or signing up. This model assumes the last interaction is the most influential in driving the conversion, highlighting which channels or campaigns close the deal. It's straightforward and widely used because it emphasizes the point of conversion, but it can overlook the importance of earlier marketing efforts that helped nurture and educate the lead along the way. As a result, last-click attribution often undervalues upper-funnel activities like brand awareness or lead generation, so it's best used alongside other attribution models to get a more complete picture of your marketing impact.

- **Linear Attribution:** Linear attribution evenly distributes credit for a conversion across all the touchpoints a customer interacts with throughout their buyer journey. Instead of favoring the first or last interaction, this model recognizes that every marketing effort—from initial awareness to final engagement—plays a role in driving the conversion. By assigning equal weight to each touchpoint, linear attribution provides a more balanced view of how different channels and campaigns contribute to success. This helps marketers understand the collective impact of their strategies and optimize across the entire funnel rather than focusing solely on specific stages. However, it may sometimes oversimplify the influence of certain key interactions by treating all touchpoints as equally important.

- **Time-decay Attribution:** Time-decay attribution assigns more credit to touchpoints that occur closer in time to the conversion, giving greater weight to the most recent interactions while still acknowledging earlier ones. This model reflects the idea that as prospects move through the funnel, the actions they take closer to the purchase decision have a stronger influence on converting. By emphasizing recent engagements, time-decay attribution helps marketers identify which channels or campaigns are most effective at closing deals, while still valuing the contribution of awareness and nurturing activities. It offers a nuanced view that balances the importance of the entire customer journey with the reality that the last few touchpoints often have the greatest impact.

- **Data-driven Attribution:** Data-driven attribution leverages machine learning algorithms to analyze your specific customer journey data and assign credit to each touchpoint based on its actual impact on conversions. Unlike rule-based models (like first-click or linear), this approach uses advanced statistical methods to understand how different interactions—such as ads, emails, or organic visits—work together to influence buying decisions. It dynamically weighs the importance of each touchpoint by examining patterns across thousands of conversion paths, providing a highly accurate and customized attribution model tailored to your business. This allows marketers to optimize budget allocation and strategy with deeper insights into which channels and tactics truly drive results, making data-driven attribution one of the most sophisticated and effective methods for measuring marketing performance.

Choosing the right model impacts how ROI is interpreted.

5. ROI and ROAS: Calculating the Return

Measuring the financial success of digital marketing efforts hinges on two critical metrics: Return on Investment (ROI) and Return on Ad Spend (ROAS). ROI evaluates the overall profitability of a campaign by comparing the net profit to the total investment. It answers the fundamental question: "Did this campaign generate more money than it cost?" ROAS, on the other hand, specifically focuses on advertising efficiency, calculated by dividing the revenue generated from ads by the amount spent on those ads. For example, a ROAS of 4:1 means that for every ₹1 spent on advertising, ₹4 was earned in revenue. While ROI provides a broad view of profitability, ROAS offers a more immediate insight into ad performance. Together, these metrics help marketers assess effectiveness, justify budget allocations, and prioritize high-performing strategies. Accurate tracking of costs and revenues is key to ensuring these figures truly reflect campaign impact.

Return on Investment (ROI)

Formula:

$$\text{ROI} = \frac{\text{Net Profit from Campaign} - \text{Cost of Campaign}}{\text{Cost of Campaign}} \times 100$$

It measures overall profitability and helps justify marketing spend.

Return on Ad Spend (ROAS)

Formula:

$$\text{ROAS} = \frac{\text{Revenue Attributed to Ads}}{\text{Cost of Ads}}$$

ROAS is particularly important in paid media to evaluate efficiency.

6. Analyzing Campaign Performance

Analyzing campaign performance involves digging into the data to understand what worked, what didn't, and why. This step goes beyond surface-level metrics like clicks and impressions to examine deeper indicators such as conversion rates, engagement patterns, and audience segments. Marketers compare performance against predefined KPIs and goals to assess success and identify gaps. For example, a high click-through rate with a low conversion rate might signal weak landing page content or targeting issues. Performance analysis should be done both during and after a campaign, allowing for real-time adjustments and post-campaign insights. Tools like Google Analytics, ad platforms, and data dashboards make it possible to track trends over time, uncover bottlenecks, and refine strategy. Ultimately, this analysis transforms raw data into actionable intelligence, enabling smarter decisions and better outcomes in future campaigns.

Beyond metrics, campaign analysis should answer:

- Which channels drove the most valuable traffic?
- What messaging or creatives performed best?
- Were the goals achieved cost-effectively?
- What can be improved in future campaigns?

Use dashboards and visualization tools like Google Data Studio, Tableau, or Power BI for clear reporting.

7. Challenges in Measuring ROI

Measuring ROI in digital marketing can be deceptively complex. One major challenge lies in tracking the entire customer journey across multiple devices, platforms, and touchpoints — which may not all be easily attributable. For instance, a user might first interact with a brand on social media, later click a search ad, and finally convert via email — making it difficult to assign credit accurately. Incomplete or inconsistent data, especially in the absence of integrated tools or proper tagging, can also skew ROI calculations. Privacy regulations like GDPR further restrict tracking, limiting visibility into user behavior. Additionally, non-revenue-generating goals such as brand awareness or engagement are harder to quantify in monetary terms, making ROI less straightforward. Lastly, delayed conversions — common in B2B or high-value purchases — can cause time lags between campaign spend and measurable return. Overcoming these challenges requires a strong analytics infrastructure, cross-channel attribution models, and a long-term view of marketing impact.

- **Multi-touch complexity:** Multi-touch complexity refers to the reality that customers rarely convert after a single interaction; instead, they engage with multiple marketing channels and touchpoints throughout their buyer journey before making a purchase or completing a desired action. These touchpoints can include organic search, paid ads, social media, email campaigns, direct visits, and more, often in varying sequences and frequencies. This complexity makes it challenging to accurately attribute credit to individual channels, as each contributes differently to awareness, consideration, and conversion stages. Understanding multi-touch complexity is essential for marketers to evaluate the full customer journey, avoid overvaluing or undervaluing specific channels, and allocate budgets more effectively across the entire marketing mix. It's why sophisticated attribution models—like data-driven or time-decay—are often necessary to capture the true influence of each interaction in a multi-channel environment.

- **Cross-device behavior:** Cross-device behavior refers to how users often interact with a brand across multiple devices—like smartphones, tablets, laptops, or desktops—during their customer journey. This creates a tracking challenge because it can be difficult to accurately identify and connect these interactions to the same individual when they switch devices. For example, a user might first discover a product on their phone, research it later on a laptop, and finally make a purchase on a desktop. Without reliable cross-device tracking, marketers risk fragmented data, leading to under- or over-attribution of conversions and an incomplete understanding of the customer journey. Solutions like user login tracking, device graph technologies, and advanced analytics platforms aim to bridge these gaps, but privacy regulations and technical limitations still make cross-device measurement one of the more complex challenges in digital marketing.

- **Offline conversions:** Offline conversions refer to valuable customer actions that happen outside of digital channels—such as in-store purchases, phone calls, or face-to-face meetings—which aren't automatically tracked by online analytics tools. Because a significant portion of sales or leads can occur offline, relying solely on digital data risks underestimating the true return on investment (ROI) of marketing efforts. For example, a user might research a product online but complete the purchase in a physical store, or a lead generated through a web form might be converted by a sales rep via phone. To capture these offline conversions, businesses often integrate CRM systems, call tracking, or point-of-sale data with their digital campaigns, enabling more complete attribution and a clearer picture of marketing effectiveness. Recognizing offline conversions is crucial for making informed budget decisions and understanding the full impact of both online and offline marketing activities.

- **Data privacy and cookie restrictions:** Data privacy regulations (like GDPR and CCPA) and increasing cookie restrictions—such as browser limitations on third-party cookies—have significantly impacted the accuracy and scope of digital tracking. These measures are designed to protect user privacy by limiting the amount of personal data marketers can collect and how it's used, but they also reduce the ability to track users across websites and devices with traditional methods. As a result, marketers face challenges in accurately attributing conversions, understanding customer journeys, and targeting ads effectively. This shift pushes the industry toward adopting privacy-friendly solutions like first-party data collection, server-side tracking, contextual advertising, and relying more on aggregated or modeled data rather than individual user-level tracking. Navigating these restrictions requires balancing compliance with maintaining actionable insights to optimize marketing performance in a privacy-conscious world.

Mitigating these challenges requires holistic tracking and first-party data strategies.

8. Best Practices for Campaign Measurement

Effective campaign measurement hinges on following key best practices that ensure accuracy, clarity, and actionable insight. First, start with clear goals and KPIs aligned with business objectives — whether it's conversions, brand lift, or engagement. Use consistent tracking methods, such as UTM parameters and event tagging, to maintain data integrity across all channels. Integrate analytics tools like Google Analytics, CRM systems, and ad platforms to create a centralized view of performance. Apply multi-touch attribution models to better understand the full customer journey rather than relying on last-click data. Regularly segment your audience and analyze performance across different demographics, devices, and behaviors to identify what resonates best. Incorporate A/B testing to validate assumptions and refine strategies. Most importantly, schedule routine performance reviews and be ready to pivot based on real-time data. These practices help marketers not only track outcomes but also continuously improve campaign effectiveness.

- Define goals before campaign launch.
- Set up tracking (UTMs, pixels, events) properly.
- Test and optimize throughout the campaign.
- Integrate cross-channel data sources.
- Align analytics with business outcomes, not just vanity metrics.

Conclusion

Digital campaign measurement and ROI analysis are at the heart of performance marketing. In a competitive and data-driven environment, the ability to quantify impact, optimize strategies, and drive continuous improvement can set successful marketers apart. Understanding your numbers isn't optional — it's the language of modern marketing success.

CHAPTER TEN

Listening and Sentiment Analysis

Introduction

In the digital era, conversations about brands, products, and services unfold publicly across social media, forums, blogs, and reviews. Businesses that ignore this dialogue risk missing critical insights. That's where social listening and sentiment analysis come into play. These tools empower marketers to go beyond surface-level metrics and tap into the emotions, opinions, and needs of their audience in real-time.

This chapter explores what listening and sentiment analysis entail, the tools involved, methodologies used, and how organizations can turn insights into action.

Unlocking Stakeholder Insights

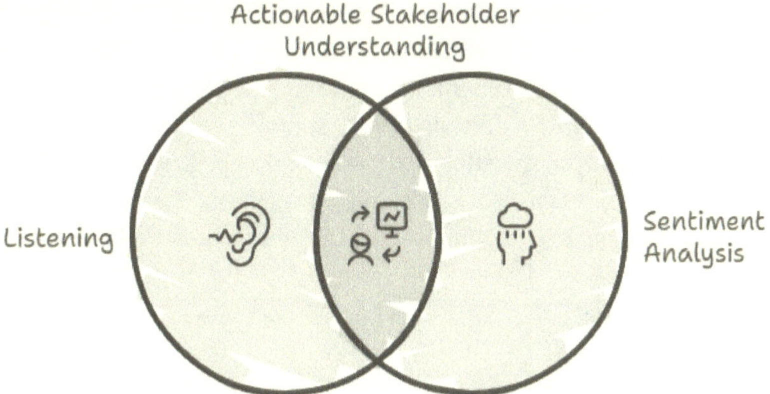

1. What is Social Listening?

Social listening is the process of monitoring digital conversations to understand what customers are saying about a brand, competitors, industry trends, or specific topics.

Social listening is the process of monitoring digital conversations to understand what customers are saying about a brand, product, industry, or topic across social media and online platforms. Unlike basic social media monitoring, which tracks metrics like mentions and engagement, social listening dives deeper to analyze the sentiment, context, and trends behind the conversations. It helps marketers identify emerging issues, measure brand perception, gather competitive intelligence, and discover opportunities to engage authentically with audiences. By capturing real-time feedback and emotional tone, social listening enables brands to respond proactively, tailor messaging, and make data-driven decisions that align with audience expectations.

It goes beyond simple keyword tracking — it's about understanding the context, tone, and intent behind the conversations.

Uses of social listening:

Social listening serves as a powerful tool for businesses across various functions. Brand monitoring is one of its primary uses, allowing companies to track mentions and gauge public sentiment about their brand in real time. It helps in reputation management by identifying potential crises early and enabling timely responses. Marketers use social listening to understand audience preferences, identify content themes that resonate, and tailor campaigns accordingly. It also offers competitive intelligence, revealing what customers are saying about competitors — their strengths, weaknesses, and gaps to exploit. In product development, social listening uncovers customer pain points and unmet needs, guiding innovation and feature improvements. Additionally, it supports customer service by flagging complaints or questions that may not be directed at a brand's official channels. Overall, social listening transforms unstructured social chatter into strategic insight, giving brands a customer-centric edge.

- Brand monitoring
- Crisis detection
- Competitor analysis
- Audience research
- Campaign feedback

- Product development input

2. Sentiment Analysis: Understanding Emotion in Data

Sentiment analysis (also called opinion mining) uses natural language processing (NLP) and machine learning to identify and extract subjective information from text.

Sentiment analysis is a core function of social listening that interprets the emotional tone behind online conversations and content. By using natural language processing (NLP) and machine learning, sentiment analysis categorizes social media posts, comments, reviews, and other digital content as positive, negative, or neutral. This helps marketers move beyond surface-level metrics to grasp how people actually feel about a brand, campaign, or issue. For instance, a spike in mentions might look promising, but sentiment analysis reveals whether those mentions reflect praise or criticism. It enables brands to track shifts in public mood, assess the impact of product launches or crises, and fine-tune messaging based on emotional resonance. In essence, sentiment analysis provides the emotional "why" behind the data, helping brands build more empathetic, responsive, and effective communication strategies.

It classifies content into categories such as:

- Positive
- Negative
- Neutral

Advanced systems can detect emotions (joy, anger, sadness), intensity, and even sarcasm.

3. Tools for Listening and Sentiment Analysis

To effectively gather insights from online conversations, businesses rely on specialized tools for social listening and sentiment analysis. Platforms like Brandwatch, Talkwalker, and Sprout Social offer comprehensive listening capabilities that track mentions across social networks, blogs, forums, and news sites. Tools such as Hootsuite Insights, powered by Brandwatch, enable real-time tracking of brand sentiment and engagement trends. Meltwater and Mention help monitor keywords, hashtags, and competitor activity, while NetBase Quid and Awario offer deep sentiment analysis with AI-driven emotional intelligence. Many of these platforms not only collect and classify data but also visualize trends, detect sentiment fluctuations, and alert teams to spikes in negative chatter. These tools are essential for brands aiming to stay ahead of public opinion, improve customer experience, and make proactive, data-driven decisions.

Numerous tools offer robust listening and sentiment features, including:

- Brandwatch
- Sprout Social
- Hootsuite Insights
- Talkwalker
- Mention
- Meltwater
- Google Alerts (basic listening)
- Lexalytics / MonkeyLearn (for advanced sentiment analysis)
- Social platforms' native analytics (Meta, X/Twitter, LinkedIn, etc.)

These tools collect data from public sources and apply AI models to interpret sentiment, trends, and volume.

4. How Listening Works: From Data to Insight

Social listening operates through a systematic process that transforms vast streams of unstructured online data into actionable insights. It begins with data collection, where tools scrape mentions, keywords, hashtags, and brand references from sources like social media platforms, blogs, forums, and news sites. This raw data is then filtered and cleaned to remove spam, duplicates, or irrelevant chatter. Next, natural language processing (NLP) and machine learning algorithms analyze the text to detect context, tone, and sentiment — identifying whether the conversation is positive, negative, or neutral. These insights are then categorized by themes, such as product feedback, customer service issues, or trending topics. Finally, the findings are visualized through dashboards and reports, enabling marketers to identify patterns, monitor sentiment shifts, and make strategic decisions. This journey from data to insight ensures that brands not only hear what's being said but also understand the underlying emotions and implications — turning social noise into business value.

The process typically involves:

- **Keyword Setup:** Keyword setup involves identifying and defining a set of specific terms and phrases that you want to monitor and target across your marketing efforts. This typically includes your brand names and variations, relevant hashtags, and competitor keywords to track industry trends and benchmarking. By carefully selecting these keywords, you can optimize SEO content, pay-per-click campaigns, and social listening efforts to ensure you're capturing relevant traffic and conversations. Monitoring competitor terms helps you understand their positioning and identify opportunities to differentiate your messaging. Additionally, including industry-specific jargon and high-intent search phrases allows you to align your content with what your audience is actively searching for. A well-planned keyword setup lays the foundation for effective targeting, measurement, and ongoing optimization across channels.

- **Data Collection:** Data collection through crawling public data sources in real time involves using automated tools or bots to scan and gather information from publicly accessible websites, social media platforms, forums, news sites, and other online repositories. This process allows marketers and analysts to capture up-to-date data such as competitor pricing, customer reviews, trending topics, or sentiment analysis without manual effort. Real-time crawling ensures that insights reflect the most current market conditions and consumer behaviors, enabling faster, more informed decision-making. However, it's important to respect website terms of service and privacy laws when collecting data, and to manage the volume and frequency of crawls to avoid overloading servers or collecting irrelevant information. When done responsibly, real-time data crawling is a powerful way to augment traditional data sources and enhance competitive intelligence.

- **Filtering:** Filtering is the crucial process of removing spam, noise, and irrelevant mentions from your collected data to ensure that your analysis and insights are accurate and meaningful. When monitoring online conversations, social media, or other public data sources, raw data often includes off-topic content, automated spam messages, or irrelevant references that can distort understanding of audience sentiment or campaign performance. Effective filtering uses keyword rules, natural language processing (NLP), sentiment analysis, and manual review to exclude these distractions. This not only improves the quality of reports and dashboards but also helps focus your marketing efforts on genuine, actionable feedback and trends. By consistently applying filtering, you maintain cleaner data sets that provide clearer, more reliable insights to guide strategy.

- **Analysis:** Analysis leveraging natural language processing (NLP) enables marketers to automatically extract meaningful insights from large volumes of unstructured text data, such as social media posts, reviews, or customer feedback. NLP techniques help identify topics and themes by grouping related words and phrases, revealing what subjects or conversations are most prevalent. Sentiment analysis further classifies this content by detecting the emotional tone—positive, negative, or neutral—offering a deeper understanding of how audiences feel about your brand, products, or campaigns. By combining topic modeling and sentiment analysis, you gain a nuanced picture of customer perceptions, emerging trends, and potential issues in real time. This empowers data-driven decision-making, allowing you to tailor messaging, improve products, or respond proactively to public sentiment. NLP-driven analysis transforms raw text into actionable intelligence at scale.

- **Visualization & Reporting:** Visualization and reporting are essential steps in turning complex data and analysis into clear, actionable insights that stakeholders can easily understand and act upon. By presenting information through dashboards and reports, marketers can highlight key metrics, trends, and patterns using charts, graphs, heatmaps, and other visual tools. Interactive dashboards allow real-time monitoring and exploration of data across different dimensions—such as time periods, channels, or audience segments—enabling quick identification of opportunities or issues. Regular reports summarize performance against goals, campaign outcomes, and insights from data analysis, providing a narrative that connects the numbers to business objectives. Effective visualization and reporting make data accessible, support strategic decision-making, and foster alignment across marketing, sales, and leadership teams.

5. Applications of Sentiment and Listening

Sentiment analysis and social listening offer a wide range of practical applications that enhance marketing, customer service, product development, and brand management. For marketers, these tools help refine messaging, tailor content strategies, and optimize campaign timing based on how audiences are reacting in real time. In customer service, social listening allows brands to detect and respond to complaints or praise quickly, often before the customer reaches out directly. Product teams can use sentiment insights to gather unfiltered feedback, helping improve features or address recurring issues. In times of crisis or controversy, sentiment tracking enables reputation management, alerting teams to rising negativity and guiding responsive communication. Additionally, companies can monitor competitor sentiment, uncovering market opportunities and benchmarking their brand against industry peers. Overall, sentiment and listening tools transform public opinion into a strategic asset — giving businesses the power to listen, learn, and lead more effectively.

Brand Health Monitoring

Brand health monitoring refers to the ongoing evaluation of how a brand is perceived by its audience, stakeholders, and the broader market. Leveraging social listening tools, sentiment analysis, and digital metrics, businesses can track vital indicators such as brand sentiment, awareness, trust, share of voice, and engagement. These metrics help paint a real-time picture of brand reputation across platforms like social media, news outlets, forums, and review sites. Monitoring brand health allows marketers to detect early warning signs of dissatisfaction, uncover recurring issues, and measure the impact of marketing campaigns or public relations efforts. It also enables competitive benchmarking, showing how a brand performs relative to rivals in terms of public perception. Importantly, consistent tracking provides actionable insights that guide messaging, product development, and customer service strategies. In today's fast-paced digital world, where consumer opinions can shift rapidly, brand health monitoring ensures that organizations stay agile, responsive, and aligned with public expectations.

Campaign Impact Assessment

Campaign impact assessment involves analyzing how audiences emotionally and behaviorally respond to marketing efforts in real-time. Beyond impressions and clicks, this process taps into sentiment analysis and engagement data to uncover how a campaign resonates with its intended audience. Using tools like social listening platforms, comment tracking, and reaction metrics, marketers can measure whether a campaign is generating positive buzz, evoking emotional responses, or sparking conversations. This insight is especially valuable during live or time-sensitive campaigns, such as product launches, brand announcements, or social causes. Real-time feedback enables agile adjustments — whether it's refining messaging, targeting, or creative assets — to maximize impact while minimizing potential backlash. By understanding emotional reactions alongside hard performance data, brands gain a holistic view of success and can ensure their marketing strategies connect authentically and effectively with their audience.

Crisis Management

In the digital age, a brand crisis can escalate within hours — or even minutes. Crisis management through social listening and analytics enables early detection of sudden negative sentiment spikes, abnormal engagement patterns, or viral backlash. By continuously monitoring conversations across social platforms, forums, and media outlets, brands can identify brewing issues before they spiral out of control. These early warning signs — such as a surge in negative mentions or emotionally charged comments — trigger alerts that allow communication teams to respond swiftly with transparency, empathy, and corrective action. Timely responses not only contain reputational damage but can also strengthen brand credibility when handled well. Furthermore, data from past crises can be used to develop proactive strategies, refine messaging, and train teams for future scenarios. In essence, real-time analytics transforms crisis management from reactive firefighting to proactive brand protection.

Product Feedback

Social listening provides a goldmine of authentic, unsolicited product feedback that traditional surveys often miss. By analyzing organic conversations across platforms like Twitter, Reddit, YouTube comments, and review sites, brands can uncover what users genuinely love, dislike, or wish was different about a product. These insights include common frustrations, feature requests, performance critiques, and even surprising use cases — all shared in real time and often in the customer's own words. Because the data comes from unfiltered, natural interactions, it offers a more accurate reflection of customer sentiment than prompted feedback. This allows product teams to prioritize updates, fix recurring issues, or enhance features that resonate with users. Listening to this kind of candid feedback also signals that a brand values its community, creating a loop of continuous improvement fueled by real user voices.

Competitor Intelligence

Social listening isn't just about monitoring your own brand — it's also a powerful tool for gathering competitor intelligence. By analyzing what people are saying about rival products, services, or campaigns, marketers can uncover strengths to learn from and weaknesses to exploit. This includes tracking sentiment, customer complaints, praise, feature mentions, and emerging trends linked to competitors. Are their users frustrated with a lack of functionality you offer? Are their campaigns generating buzz — or backlash? These insights help businesses benchmark performance, anticipate market shifts, and fine-tune positioning. Moreover, by identifying unmet needs or dissatisfaction in the competitor's customer base, brands can spot strategic opportunities to attract switchers and deliver better experiences. In short, competitor intelligence gathered through listening turns market noise into actionable competitive advantage.

Influencer Identification

In the age of digital word-of-mouth, influencer identification is crucial for amplifying brand reach and credibility. Social listening enables marketers to go beyond follower counts and pinpoint real influence — identifying individuals who consistently spark conversations, shape opinions, and drive engagement within a specific niche. These could be bloggers, industry experts, content creators, or even passionate customers whose voices carry weight in targeted communities. By analyzing metrics like engagement rates, sentiment around their posts, and the virality of their content, brands can select influencers who align with their values and truly resonate with their audience. Partnering with such individuals not only enhances campaign effectiveness but also helps cultivate authentic brand advocacy, grounded in relevance and trust.

6. Challenges and Limitations

While social listening and sentiment analysis offer powerful insights, they come with notable challenges and limitations. One major hurdle is sarcasm and irony detection — even advanced AI systems often misinterpret sarcastic remarks, classifying negative sentiments as positive (or vice versa). Multilingual accuracy is another issue, as sentiment models tend to be trained primarily on English, making them less reliable when analyzing text in other languages or dialects. Additionally, there's context loss: algorithms can struggle to understand nuanced meanings or the cultural and situational factors that influence sentiment, leading to oversimplified interpretations. Lastly, the sheer volume of online content introduces noise in data — not every mention is relevant or actionable, and sifting through this clutter to extract valuable insights requires careful filtering and human oversight. These challenges highlight the importance of combining automated tools with strategic human analysis to ensure meaningful outcomes.

- **Sarcasm and Irony Detection:** Sarcasm and irony detection remains a significant challenge for AI because these forms of expression rely heavily on tone, context, and cultural cues that are often subtle and nuanced. While natural language processing models have improved, they still frequently misclassify sarcastic or ironic statements—interpreting them literally rather than recognizing the intended opposite meaning. This can lead to inaccurate sentiment analysis, such as tagging a sarcastic compliment as genuinely positive or a humorous complaint as negative. Improving sarcasm detection requires more advanced context understanding, including recognizing linguistic cues, user behavior patterns, and even multimodal signals like emojis or voice tone in some cases. Until AI can consistently grasp these complexities, marketers and analysts should approach automated sentiment results with caution and consider supplementing them with human review for more accurate insights.

- **Multilingual Accuracy:** Multilingual accuracy is a common challenge in sentiment analysis because models trained primarily on one language—often English—may struggle to understand the nuances, idioms, and cultural context of other languages. This can lead to poorer performance when analyzing sentiment in non-English content, resulting in misclassifications or oversimplified interpretations. Different languages express emotions and sarcasm differently, and direct translations don't always capture the intended meaning. To improve multilingual accuracy, models need to be trained on diverse, language-specific datasets and incorporate cultural context. Additionally, leveraging native speakers for validation or combining machine learning with rule-based approaches can help enhance reliability across languages. Without these considerations, insights drawn from multilingual data may be incomplete or misleading.

- **Context Loss:** Context loss occurs when AI models analyzing sentiment fail to fully understand the surrounding circumstances or nuances that influence the meaning of a statement. Sentiment can dramatically change depending on factors like prior conversations, cultural background, industry jargon, or even subtle humor and sarcasm. Machines often process text in isolated chunks without the broader context, leading to misinterpretation—for example, a phrase that's positive in one setting might be negative in another. This limitation means that automated sentiment analysis can sometimes provide inaccurate or overly simplistic results. To mitigate context loss, it's important to incorporate more sophisticated models that consider dialogue history, user profiles, or situational cues, and to complement AI insights with human judgment when interpreting complex or ambiguous data.

- **Noise in Data:** Noise in data refers to the presence of irrelevant, misleading, or low-quality information within your collected datasets—such as off-topic mentions, spam, duplicate content, or random chatter—that doesn't contribute meaningful insights. In marketing and social listening, this noise can obscure important trends, distort sentiment analysis, and make it harder to identify genuine customer feedback or campaign impact. Filtering and cleaning data are essential steps to reduce noise, ensuring that your analysis focuses on relevant and valuable mentions that truly reflect audience opinions and behavior. Managing noise effectively improves the accuracy of insights, enhances decision-making, and helps marketers prioritize efforts based on quality data rather than being overwhelmed by irrelevant information.

Despite these, evolving AI models are improving accuracy and context detection over time.

7. Best Practices for Effective Listening

Effective social listening goes beyond passively monitoring mentions—it requires a strategic, consistent, and purposeful approach. Start by defining clear objectives: Are you tracking customer satisfaction, spotting crises early, or researching competitors? Align your listening goals with broader marketing and business priorities. Use precise and dynamic keyword sets, including branded terms, common misspellings, hashtags, and industry jargon to ensure comprehensive coverage. Incorporate filters for language, geography, and sentiment to narrow down relevant insights. Combine quantitative data with qualitative context—understanding the 'why' behind the sentiment is key. Choose tools that integrate with your CRM, analytics, and campaign platforms to connect insights to action. Regularly audit your listening setup to refine parameters and eliminate noise. Most importantly, develop a process to act on insights—share findings across departments, respond in real time, and continuously evolve your brand based on authentic audience feedback.

- **Define Clear Objectives:** Defining clear objectives is the foundational step in any data-driven marketing or analytics effort. It means precisely identifying what you want to measure and why—whether that's tracking brand mentions to gauge awareness, collecting campaign feedback to assess effectiveness, monitoring product issues to improve quality, or any other specific goal. Clear objectives help focus data collection, analysis, and reporting efforts on the most relevant metrics and insights, preventing wasted resources on irrelevant information. They also provide a benchmark for success and guide decision-making, ensuring that every action is aligned with your overall business and marketing strategy. Without well-defined objectives, it's challenging to interpret data meaningfully or demonstrate the impact of your initiatives.

- **Use Boolean Searches:** Using Boolean searches involves applying logical operators like AND, OR, NOT, and parentheses to create precise and refined queries when collecting or monitoring data. This technique helps filter out irrelevant mentions and hone in on the most relevant content by combining or excluding specific keywords, phrases, or conditions. For example, a Boolean search like ("brand name" OR "product name") AND NOT "unrelated term" ensures that you capture all mentions related to your brand or product while excluding topics that might clutter your results. By carefully crafting Boolean queries, you improve the quality of your data, reduce noise, and make analysis more efficient and accurate—allowing you to focus on insights that truly matter to your objectives.

- **Combine Quantitative and Qualitative Insights:** Combining quantitative and qualitative insights means blending hard data—like metrics, statistics, and trends—with the rich, detailed stories behind those numbers, such as customer opinions, emotions, and motivations. Quantitative data tells you what is happening (e.g., how many people mentioned your brand or clicked on an ad), while qualitative insights explain why it's happening (e.g., how customers feel about your product or the reasons behind their behavior). When you integrate both types of insights, you get a fuller, more nuanced understanding of your audience and campaign performance. This combination helps marketers develop smarter, more empathetic strategies that are grounded in evidence but also deeply connected to real customer experiences—ultimately leading to more effective messaging, product improvements, and business growth.

- **Track Over Time:** Tracking data over time is essential because one-off snapshots only provide a limited, momentary view of performance or sentiment, which can be misleading or incomplete. By monitoring trends, patterns, and changes across days, weeks, or months, you gain a clearer understanding of how campaigns evolve, how audience perceptions shift, and how seasonality or external events impact your results. Continuous tracking helps identify long-term growth opportunities, recurring issues, and the sustained effects of marketing efforts, enabling more strategic planning and timely adjustments. Without this ongoing perspective, decisions may be based on isolated data points rather than the bigger picture, increasing the risk of misinterpretation and missed opportunities.

- **Act on Insights:** Acting on insights is crucial because collecting and analyzing data alone doesn't drive results—insights must lead to informed decisions and tangible actions to create real value. Without applying what you learn, valuable information remains unused, and opportunities for improvement, optimization, or innovation are missed. Whether it's adjusting a campaign, refining messaging, addressing customer pain points, or reallocating budget, turning insights into action closes the loop between data and business outcomes. A culture that prioritizes responsiveness and agility ensures that data-driven insights translate into continuous growth, better customer experiences, and stronger competitive advantage. In short, insights without action are simply wasted data.

8. Case Example

Example: Coca-Cola's Real-Time Listening During Campaigns

Coca-Cola uses social listening to monitor real-time consumer feedback during large campaigns like the Super Bowl or Olympics. When sentiment drops or a trending complaint emerges, their team adjusts messaging or engages with customers instantly — turning potential backlash into brand wins.

Conclusion

Listening and sentiment analysis are no longer optional — they are vital components of a responsive, customer-centric digital marketing strategy. They transform vast volumes of unstructured data into actionable insights, enabling brands to understand not just what people are saying, but how they feel about it.

In a noisy online world, those who listen closely and understand deeply hold the competitive edge.

CHAPTER ELEVEN

Competitive Intelligence and Benchmarking

Introduction

In the fast-moving digital landscape, understanding your brand in isolation is no longer enough. To stay ahead, businesses must continually observe, analyze, and respond to their competitive environment. Competitive intelligence (CI) and benchmarking are two powerful techniques that enable marketers to gain strategic insight, identify market opportunities, and measure performance against industry standards.

This chapter explores the principles, tools, methods, and real-world application of competitive intelligence and benchmarking in digital marketing.

1. What is Competitive Intelligence?

Competitive Intelligence (CI) refers to the process of gathering, analyzing, and interpreting data about competitors, market trends, customer behavior, and industry developments to support strategic decision-making.

Unlike espionage, CI is ethical and based on publicly available data.

Goals of CI in Digital Marketing:

- Monitor competitor campaigns and performance.
- Discover gaps in market offerings.
- Understand consumer sentiment toward competitors.
- Anticipate market shifts or new entrants.
- Enhance product positioning and messaging.

2. What is Benchmarking?

Benchmarking is the practice of comparing your brand's digital performance against competitors or industry standards to evaluate effectiveness. Benchmarking is the strategic practice of comparing a brand's digital performance—such as website traffic, user engagement, conversion rates, and social media metrics—against competitors or industry standards to assess effectiveness. This process helps organizations identify performance gaps, uncover opportunities for improvement, and adopt best practices from high-performing peers. Benchmarking can take various forms, including competitive benchmarking (comparing with direct rivals), industry benchmarking (measuring against broader industry norms), and internal benchmarking (evaluating performance across different departments or time periods within the same organization). Ultimately, benchmarking supports data-driven decision-making and fosters continuous improvement in digital strategy and execution.

It answers questions like:

- How does our website traffic compare?
- Are we getting similar engagement on social media?
- What's our average email open rate vs. the industry?
- Are our paid ads more or less efficient than peers?

Types of Benchmarking:

- **Competitive Benchmarking:** Competitive Benchmarking is the process of comparing your brand's performance directly against that of your key competitors. It focuses on evaluating metrics such as market share, website traffic, social media engagement, customer satisfaction, and overall digital presence. By analyzing how direct competitors perform in similar areas, businesses can identify strengths, weaknesses, and opportunities to improve their own strategies. This type of benchmarking helps organizations stay competitive, refine their value proposition, and make informed strategic decisions based on real-world market dynamics.

- **Industry Benchmarking:** Industry Benchmarking involves comparing your brand's performance metrics—such as conversion rates, customer engagement, ROI, or operational efficiency—against the average standards or best practices within your broader industry or sector. Unlike competitive benchmarking, which focuses on direct rivals, industry benchmarking provides a wider view by highlighting how your organization measures up to general market norms. This helps identify whether your performance is aligned with, lagging behind, or exceeding industry expectations. It also supports strategic planning by offering context for goal setting, resource allocation, and identifying emerging trends that may impact the entire sector.

- **Internal Benchmarking:** Internal Benchmarking is the process of comparing performance metrics across different departments, teams, business units, or time periods within the same organization. Rather than looking outward at competitors or industry standards, it focuses on identifying best practices and performance variations internally. This approach helps uncover operational inefficiencies, set realistic goals, and foster knowledge sharing across the organization. It is particularly useful for tracking progress over time, ensuring consistency, and driving continuous improvement based on internal successes.

3. Sources and Tools for Competitive Intelligence

Sources and Tools for Competitive Intelligence encompass a wide range of platforms and techniques used to gather, analyze, and interpret information about competitors and the broader market. Common sources include publicly available data such as company websites, press releases, annual reports, job postings, and news articles. Social media platforms, customer reviews, and forums also offer valuable real-time insights into brand perception and market sentiment. Additionally, specialized tools like SEMrush, Similarweb, Ahrefs, SpyFu, and Crunchbase enable businesses to monitor digital marketing strategies, website traffic, keyword rankings, backlinks, and competitor growth. Social listening tools like Brandwatch or Sprout Social, along with analytics platforms like Google Analytics and Tableau, support deeper analysis. These sources and tools collectively empower organizations to stay informed, anticipate market changes, and make strategic decisions with confidence.

Modern tools offer robust data-gathering capabilities for digital CI:

SEO and Web Traffic:

SEMrush, Ahrefs, SimilarWeb, SpyFu: Keyword gaps, backlink profiles, traffic sources. SEO and Web Traffic analysis is a vital component of competitive intelligence, offering insights into how competitors attract and retain online visitors. By examining elements such as keyword rankings, organic search performance, backlink profiles, and traffic sources, businesses can uncover the strategies that drive their competitors' visibility and engagement. Tools like SEMrush, Ahrefs, Moz, and Similarweb provide detailed reports on search engine optimization efforts, including high-performing content, domain authority, and traffic volume. Understanding these SEO and web traffic patterns allows organizations to refine their own digital strategies, improve search rankings, and capitalize on untapped opportunities in the market.

Social Media Monitoring:

BuzzSumo, Sprout Social, Brandwatch: Content performance, influencer analysis, sentiment tracking. Social Media Monitoring involves tracking competitors' activities, audience engagement, and brand sentiment across platforms like Facebook, Instagram, X (formerly Twitter), LinkedIn, and YouTube. By observing what content resonates with their followers, the frequency of posts, response times, influencer partnerships, and customer feedback, businesses can gain real-time insights into competitor strategies and audience preferences. Tools such as Brandwatch, Sprout Social, Hootsuite, and Mention help automate this process, providing analytics on engagement metrics, trending topics, and sentiment analysis. These insights support the development of more effective social campaigns and help identify gaps or opportunities in the market.

Ad Intelligence:

Moat, Adbeat, Facebook Ad Library: Monitor ad creatives, placements, frequency, and strategies. Ad Intelligence refers to the process of analyzing competitors' advertising strategies across digital channels such as search engines, social media platforms, display networks, and video ads. It involves gathering data on ad creatives, formats, placements, targeting methods, budgets, and campaign duration to understand how competitors are positioning their products or services. Tools like Meta Ad Library, Google Ads Transparency Center, Moat, Adbeat, and Similarweb Ads offer valuable insights into which ads are running, where they appear, and how they perform. By studying these patterns, businesses can identify effective messaging tactics, avoid ad fatigue, and optimize their own ad spend for better ROI.

Email Marketing Comparison:

Mailchimp, Campaign Monitor Reports: Benchmark open and click-through rates. Email Marketing Comparison involves analyzing the email campaigns of competitors to gain insights into their communication strategies, content styles, frequency, subject lines, and promotional tactics. By subscribing to competitors' newsletters or using tools like MailCharts, Owletter, and Milled, businesses can track how often emails are sent, what types of messages are used (e.g., product launches, discounts, newsletters), and how they align with seasonal trends or major campaigns. This information helps organizations benchmark their own email performance, refine their messaging, improve engagement rates, and ensure their email strategies remain competitive and customer-focused.

Review and Feedback Platforms:

G2, Trustpilot, Google Reviews: Analyze customer feedback and compare ratings. Review and Feedback Platforms provide valuable insights into customer perceptions, satisfaction levels, and pain points related to competitors' products or services. Platforms such as Google Reviews, Trustpilot, Yelp, G2, Capterra, and Amazon offer unfiltered customer feedback that can highlight strengths, weaknesses, and common complaints. Analyzing this data helps businesses identify market gaps, improve their own offerings, and tailor messaging to address unmet needs. Additionally, trends in review volume, sentiment, and responsiveness can reveal how well competitors manage customer relationships and support, offering a benchmark for enhancing your own customer experience strategy.

Custom Research:

Surveys, mystery shopping, and manual audits of competitor websites and content. Custom Research involves conducting original, tailored investigations to gather specific insights that aren't readily available through public sources or automated tools. This can include surveys, interviews, focus groups, mystery shopping, and expert consultations designed to explore customer preferences, competitor strategies, product perceptions, and emerging trends. Custom research provides depth and context to competitive intelligence efforts, enabling businesses to uncover nuanced insights and make more informed strategic decisions. While it requires more time and resources, the findings are highly targeted and can offer a significant competitive edge in areas like product development, positioning, and market entry.

4. Key Metrics for Benchmarking

Key Metrics for Benchmarking are the performance indicators used to evaluate how well a business is doing in comparison to competitors, industry standards, or internal goals. These metrics vary by area but commonly include website traffic, bounce rate, conversion rate, click-through rate (CTR), customer acquisition cost (CAC), return on investment (ROI), social media engagement, and email open and click rates. For e-commerce or service-based businesses, additional metrics like cart abandonment rate, average order value (AOV), and customer lifetime value (CLV) are also critical. Monitoring these benchmarks helps organizations identify gaps, optimize performance, and set realistic, data-driven targets that align with business objectives.

Common benchmarks include:

Area	Metrics to Benchmark
Website	Traffic, Bounce Rate, Time on Site
SEO	Keyword Rankings, Domain Authority
Paid Media	CPC, CTR, ROAS, Impressions
Social Media	Engagement Rate, Follower Growth, Reach
Email Marketing	Open Rate, CTR, Unsubscribe Rate
E-commerce	Conversion Rate, Cart Abandonment Rate
Content Marketing	Shares, Comments, Average Read Time

5. How to Conduct Competitive Benchmarking

Conducting Competitive Benchmarking involves a structured approach to evaluating your brand's performance against direct competitors. The process begins by identifying key competitors and selecting relevant performance metrics—such as website traffic, SEO rankings, social media engagement, or customer satisfaction scores. Next, data is collected using tools like SEMrush, Similarweb, Sprout Social, or customer review platforms. Once gathered, the data is analyzed to highlight performance gaps, strengths, and areas for improvement. The final step is to apply these insights to refine strategies, set realistic performance goals, and continuously monitor progress. Regular benchmarking ensures your business stays aligned with market standards and ahead of emerging trends.

- **Identify Competitors:** Identifying competitors involves selecting a focused group of 3 to 5 businesses that operate in the same market space and target similar customer segments. This group should include both direct competitors—companies offering the same or very similar products or services—and indirect competitors—those whose offerings fulfill the same customer needs in different ways. Choosing a balanced mix allows you to benchmark your performance effectively, understand market dynamics, spot emerging trends, and uncover gaps or opportunities for differentiation. A clear competitive set provides valuable context for strategic planning, enabling you to tailor your messaging, pricing, and innovation to stand out in the marketplace.

- **Select KPIs:** Selecting KPIs means choosing key performance indicators that directly align with your specific business and marketing goals. Instead of tracking every available metric, focus on those that truly measure progress toward your objectives—whether that's increasing brand awareness, driving website traffic, generating leads, boosting sales, or improving customer retention. Relevant KPIs provide clear benchmarks for success, simplify performance monitoring, and help prioritize efforts and resources effectively. By concentrating on meaningful metrics, you can quickly identify what's working, spot areas for improvement, and make data-driven decisions that move your strategy forward.

- **Collect Data:** Collecting data involves gathering relevant information using tools like analytics platforms, social listening software, CRM systems, or manual tracking methods over a defined period. Setting a clear time frame—whether daily, weekly, monthly, or tied to a campaign duration—ensures consistent and comparable data. Automated tools can efficiently capture large volumes of data from various channels, while manual tracking may be needed for niche sources or qualitative insights. Organized data collection is essential for accurate analysis, helping you observe trends, measure performance against goals, and make informed decisions based on reliable, timely information.

- **Analyze Gaps:** Analyzing gaps means comparing your performance against competitors to identify areas where they are outperforming you and where you hold a competitive advantage. This involves evaluating key metrics, customer feedback, product features, market share, and brand perception to uncover strengths, weaknesses, opportunities, and threats. Understanding these gaps helps you pinpoint what competitors do better—whether it's in pricing, customer service, innovation, or marketing—and where you excel. By clearly mapping these insights, you can develop targeted strategies to close performance gaps, capitalize on your strengths, and differentiate your brand more effectively in the market.

- **Develop Strategy:** Developing strategy based on insights means using the knowledge gained from data analysis and competitive gaps to make informed adjustments that improve your marketing and business outcomes. This could involve launching new campaigns tailored to untapped audiences, creating more relevant and engaging content that resonates with your customers, revising pricing models to stay competitive, or enhancing product features to meet market demands. By grounding strategic decisions in real insights rather than assumptions, you increase the likelihood of success, optimize resource allocation, and drive stronger results. A flexible, insight-driven strategy also enables ongoing refinement as market conditions and customer behaviors evolve.

- **Monitor Continuously:** Monitoring continuously involves establishing recurring reports or live dashboards that provide up-to-date visibility into your key metrics and campaign performance. This ongoing tracking allows you to quickly spot trends, identify issues, and measure the impact of any strategic changes in real time. By automating data collection and visualization, you save time and ensure that stakeholders have consistent access to relevant insights without delays. Continuous monitoring fosters a proactive approach, enabling timely optimizations and agile decision-making that keeps your marketing efforts aligned with your goals and responsive to shifting market conditions.

6. Ethical Considerations in CI

Ethical Considerations in Competitive Intelligence (CI) are crucial to maintaining integrity, trust, and compliance while gathering and analyzing competitor data. CI should always rely on legally and ethically sourced information, such as publicly available data, market reports, or social media content. Practices like hacking, misrepresentation, industrial espionage, or accessing confidential information without consent are unethical and often illegal. Organizations must ensure that CI activities align with industry regulations, data privacy laws (such as GDPR), and internal codes of conduct. Upholding ethical standards not only protects a company's reputation but also fosters responsible and sustainable competitive practices.

CI must always adhere to legal and ethical standards:

- Use publicly available data only.
- Do not impersonate individuals or access private systems.
- Respect competitor trademarks and copyrights.

7. Benefits of CI and Benchmarking

Competitive Intelligence (CI) and Benchmarking offer significant strategic advantages by enabling organizations to make informed, data-driven decisions. They help businesses understand their market position, identify performance gaps, and uncover emerging trends and opportunities. CI provides deep insights into competitor strategies, customer behavior, and industry shifts, while benchmarking translates those insights into measurable comparisons against competitors or industry standards. Together, they support better product development, targeted marketing, resource allocation, and risk management. Ultimately, these practices lead to improved operational efficiency, stronger competitive positioning, and sustainable business growth.

- Smarter strategy development
- Faster identification of trends and threats
- Greater innovation through gap analysis
- Improved marketing ROI
- Enhanced customer targeting

8. Real-World Application: Case Example

A leading online retail brand noticed declining customer engagement and decided to conduct competitive intelligence and benchmarking to identify the issue. Using tools like Similarweb and Sprout Social, the company analyzed its top three competitors, focusing on website traffic, SEO performance, social media activity, and customer reviews. The analysis revealed that competitors were outperforming in mobile optimization and influencer-driven social campaigns. The brand responded by revamping its mobile experience and launching a targeted influencer strategy. Within three months, it saw a 25% increase in mobile conversions and a 40% boost in social engagement, demonstrating how competitive intelligence and benchmarking can drive actionable improvements and measurable results.

Example: Nike vs. Adidas Digital Intelligence Battle

Nike and Adidas constantly benchmark each other's campaigns, social engagement, and influencer strategy. When Adidas saw Nike outperforming on Instagram Stories, they restructured their content calendar, focused on short-form storytelling, and boosted their ROI from Instagram ads by 23% in the following quarter.

9. Challenges in Competitive Intelligence

Challenges in Competitive Intelligence (CI) stem from the complexity of collecting accurate, relevant, and timely data in a constantly evolving market. One major challenge is information overload, where the sheer volume of available data can make it difficult to extract actionable insights. Data reliability is another concern, as not all sources are credible or up-to-date. Additionally, limited access to competitor information, especially proprietary or internal data, can hinder a full analysis. Ensuring ethical compliance and avoiding legal pitfalls adds another layer of complexity. Finally, interpreting CI data correctly requires analytical expertise and context, without which businesses risk drawing flawed conclusions. Overcoming these challenges requires the right tools, skilled analysts, and a disciplined CI process.

- **Data Accuracy:** Data accuracy is a critical consideration because no tool or platform guarantees perfect reliability—errors can arise from tracking limitations, technical glitches, sampling issues, or incomplete data capture. These inaccuracies can lead to misinformed decisions if not recognized and managed properly. It's important to validate data regularly, cross-check findings across multiple sources, and understand each tool's strengths and limitations. Being aware of potential inaccuracies allows marketers to interpret insights more cautiously, apply context, and avoid overreliance on any single data point. Ultimately, maintaining a focus on data quality ensures more trustworthy analysis and better-informed strategies.

- **Information Overload:** Information overload happens when you collect vast amounts of data but lack clear focus or filtering, making it difficult to identify what's truly important. This can overwhelm teams, slow decision-making, and dilute attention from key insights that drive results. To avoid this, it's essential to prioritize relevant metrics aligned with your objectives, use tools that highlight actionable trends, and apply effective data organization and visualization. By managing information overload, you ensure that your analysis remains clear, focused, and impactful—helping you make smarter, faster decisions without getting lost in unnecessary details.

- **Dynamic Landscape:** The dynamic landscape of marketing means that competitor strategies can shift rapidly due to market trends, new technologies, consumer behavior changes, or unexpected events. This constant evolution requires businesses to stay vigilant and adaptable, regularly monitoring competitor activities and industry developments. Relying on outdated insights risks falling behind, so maintaining agility through continuous analysis and flexible strategies is key. By anticipating and responding quickly to competitor moves, you can seize opportunities, mitigate threats, and maintain a strong position in a fast-changing environment.

- **Blind Spots:** Blind spots occur when critical data—such as detailed sales figures, CRM insights, or internal customer interactions—is not publicly accessible or integrated into your analysis. This lack of visibility can create gaps in understanding the full customer journey, competitive performance, or campaign effectiveness. Without this internal data, external analysis may miss important factors influencing results or fail to capture the true impact of marketing efforts. To overcome blind spots, it's important to combine publicly available data with internal systems and cross-department collaboration, ensuring a more comprehensive, accurate view that supports better decision-making and strategy development.

Conclusion

Competitive intelligence and benchmarking transform external data into strategic advantage. By understanding how your brand compares to others and keeping a pulse on competitors' moves, you position your business to adapt, innovate, and lead. In digital marketing, where trends change daily and attention is fleeting, being informed is not just useful — it's essential.

CHAPTER TWELVE

Google Analytics and Other Tools

Introduction

Data is the lifeblood of digital marketing — and tools like Google Analytics provide the clarity to act on it. Whether you're tracking website traffic, measuring campaign performance, or understanding customer behavior, analytics tools turn guesswork into strategy. This chapter introduces Google Analytics, explores its key features, and highlights other essential tools that support comprehensive digital marketing analysis.

1. What is Google Analytics?

Google Analytics (GA) is a free web analytics tool by Google that tracks and reports website traffic. It provides deep insights into how users find, interact with, and navigate through websites or mobile apps.

The latest version, Google Analytics 4 (GA4), offers advanced event-based tracking, cross-device measurement, and privacy-focused data collection.

2. Why Google Analytics Matters in Digital Marketing

Google Analytics is a cornerstone tool in digital marketing because it provides comprehensive insights into how users interact with a website or app. It tracks key metrics such as traffic sources, user behavior, bounce rates, conversion paths, and demographic information, allowing marketers to understand what's working and what isn't. By analyzing this data, businesses can make informed decisions to optimize content, refine targeting strategies, improve user experience, and maximize return on investment (ROI). Google Analytics also supports goal tracking, A/B testing, and integration with platforms like Google Ads, making it essential for measuring campaign performance and driving data-driven marketing strategies.

- **Audience Understanding:** Audience understanding involves gathering detailed information about the people who visit your website, including their demographics (age, gender, interests), geographic location, and the devices they use (mobile, desktop, tablet). This knowledge helps you tailor your marketing messages, design user experiences, and target ads more effectively to meet the specific needs and preferences of your audience. By analyzing these insights, you can identify your core customer segments, optimize content and offers for different groups, and improve overall engagement and conversion rates. Deep audience understanding is key to creating personalized, relevant experiences that drive stronger relationships and business growth.

- **Behavior Tracking:** Behavior tracking involves monitoring how users interact with your website or app by capturing actions such as page views, scroll depth, clicks, and bounce rates. This data reveals user engagement patterns, showing which content attracts attention, where visitors drop off, and how smoothly they navigate your site. Understanding these behaviors helps identify usability issues, optimize site layout, improve content relevance, and enhance the overall user experience. By analyzing behavior tracking metrics, marketers can make informed decisions to increase engagement, reduce friction, and ultimately boost conversions and customer satisfaction.

- **Acquisition Insights:** Acquisition insights focus on understanding where your website visitors are coming from by tracking traffic sources such as organic search, paid advertising, referral links, and social media channels. This information helps you identify which marketing efforts are driving the most visitors, how different channels perform in attracting your target audience, and where to allocate budget and resources for maximum impact. By analyzing acquisition data, you can optimize campaigns, improve targeting, and develop strategies that boost high-quality traffic, ultimately leading to better engagement and higher conversion rates.

- **Conversion Goals:** Conversion goals are specific actions you want users to complete on your website or app—such as making a purchase, submitting a contact form, signing up for a newsletter, or downloading a resource. Setting up and monitoring these goals in your analytics tools allows you to measure how effectively your site drives desired outcomes. Tracking conversions helps identify which campaigns, pages, or user journeys are most successful, revealing opportunities to optimize the experience and increase results. Clear conversion goals provide a focused way to evaluate performance and demonstrate the real business impact of your marketing efforts.

- **Campaign Evaluation:** Campaign evaluation involves systematically measuring and analyzing the performance of various marketing channels—such as SEO, PPC, email, social media, and content marketing—to determine how well they achieve set objectives. By tracking key metrics like traffic, engagement, conversions, and ROI for each channel, you can identify which tactics are driving success and which need improvement. This comprehensive assessment helps optimize budget allocation, refine messaging, and enhance targeting strategies. Regular campaign evaluation ensures your marketing efforts stay effective, aligned with goals, and responsive to changing audience behaviors.

- **Real-Time Reporting:** Real-time reporting allows you to monitor live user behavior as it happens during product launches, marketing campaigns, or special events. This immediate visibility helps you track key metrics like traffic spikes, user engagement, conversion rates, and any technical issues in the moment. By having up-to-the-minute data, you can quickly respond to unexpected challenges, capitalize on opportunities, and make timely optimizations to maximize campaign effectiveness. Real-time reporting empowers agile decision-making, ensuring your marketing efforts stay on track and deliver the best possible results during critical periods.

3. Key Features of Google Analytics (GA4)

Google Analytics 4 (GA4) introduces a modern, event-based data model that offers deeper insights into user behavior across websites and apps. Unlike Universal Analytics, GA4 focuses on events rather than sessions, enabling more flexible and granular tracking. Key features include cross-platform tracking, which unifies data from websites and mobile apps, enhanced measurement for automatically tracking actions like scrolls, video engagement, and outbound clicks, and AI-powered insights for predictive metrics such as purchase probability and churn risk. GA4 also offers privacy-centric controls, aligning with evolving data protection regulations, and deeper integration with Google Ads for advanced audience targeting. Its customizable reporting tools and real-time data views make GA4 a powerful platform for modern digital marketing analytics.

Feature	Description
Event-Based Model	Tracks user interactions like clicks, scrolls, video plays.
User-Centric Reporting	Measures behavior across sessions and devices.
Engagement Metrics	Tracks engaged sessions, engagement rate, time spent.
Conversion Tracking	Monitor defined user actions that contribute to business goals.
Exploration Reports	Custom, in-depth analysis using segments and funnels.
Integration with Google Ads	Connect ad spend and ROI directly to user behavior.

4. Setting Up Google Analytics

Setting up Google Analytics, particularly GA4, is a crucial first step in tracking and understanding your digital performance. The process begins by creating a Google Analytics account and setting up a new GA4 property. Once the property is created, you'll receive a Measurement ID, which needs to be added to your website using either Google Tag Manager or directly within the site's code. After integration, you can configure data streams (for websites and apps), enable enhanced measurement features, and set up conversion goals and custom events to track key actions like purchases, sign-ups, or downloads. Proper setup ensures accurate data collection, which forms the foundation for actionable insights and effective decision-making in digital marketing.

To use GA effectively:

- Create a Google Analytics account.
- Install the GA tracking code (via GTM or manual HTML insertion).
- Set up events, conversions, and audiences.
- Link with Google Ads, Search Console, and BigQuery if needed.
- Test setup using DebugView and Realtime reports.

5. Limitations of Google Analytics

While Google Analytics is a powerful tool for tracking and analyzing digital performance, it does have several limitations. One key challenge is its data sampling in standard reports, which can affect the accuracy of insights for high-traffic websites. GA4's learning curve is another concern, as its event-based model and new interface can be complex for beginners. Additionally, data privacy regulations like GDPR and CCPA have led to more restricted data collection, potentially limiting the completeness of user insights. Google Analytics also does not track personal identifiable information (PII), which can constrain detailed user profiling. Lastly, integrating and customizing reports may require technical expertise, especially when setting up advanced tracking with Google Tag Manager or BigQuery. Despite these limitations, GA remains a valuable tool when used alongside other analytics and marketing platforms.

- **Learning Curve:** The learning curve for Google Analytics 4 (GA4) can be steep, especially for beginners, because its interface and data structure differ significantly from the previous Universal Analytics version. GA4 introduces new concepts like event-based tracking, customizable reports, and a more flexible, user-centric data model, which require time to understand and navigate effectively. This complexity can initially slow down adoption and make it challenging to extract meaningful insights without proper training or experience. However, investing time to learn GA4 pays off by unlocking deeper, more granular analysis and future-proofing your analytics capabilities as Google phases out older versions.

- **Data Sampling:** Data sampling occurs when analytics tools process only a subset of a large dataset to generate reports faster, rather than analyzing every single data point. While this speeds up processing, it can reduce the precision and accuracy of your insights because the sampled data may not perfectly represent the full dataset. This is especially common with very large traffic volumes or complex queries in tools like Google Analytics. Sampling can lead to slight discrepancies in metrics, making it harder to rely on exact numbers for critical decisions. To minimize its impact, you can use shorter date ranges, simplify reports, or leverage premium analytics solutions that offer unsampled data. Being aware of sampling helps ensure more trustworthy analysis and better-informed strategies.

- **Cookie Reliance:** Cookie reliance refers to the dependence on browser cookies to track user behavior, which faces increasing challenges due to stricter privacy regulations and browser policies limiting cookie usage. With measures like third-party cookie blocking and consent requirements, it's becoming harder to collect comprehensive tracking data, leading to gaps in user journeys and less accurate attribution. This shift forces marketers to adopt alternative tracking methods such as first-party data collection, server-side tracking, and contextual advertising. Understanding the limits of cookie-based tracking is essential for adapting measurement strategies to maintain effective audience insights and campaign performance in a privacy-conscious landscape.

- **Lack of Heatmaps or Session Recordings:** The lack of built-in heatmaps or session recordings in many analytics platforms means you often need to integrate with specialized third-party tools to gain deeper insights into user behavior. Heatmaps visually show where users click, scroll, or hover on your site, while session recordings let you watch real user interactions in real time. Without these features, understanding the "why" behind user actions can be challenging, limiting your ability to identify usability issues or optimize the user experience. Integrating complementary tools helps fill this gap, providing richer behavioral data that supports more effective website improvements and conversion optimization.

6. Other Essential Digital Analytics Tools

While Google Analytics is widely used, several other digital analytics tools offer complementary or specialized capabilities that enhance data-driven marketing. Adobe Analytics provides robust real-time data analysis and customization for enterprise-level needs. Hotjar and Microsoft Clarity offer visual behavior tracking through heatmaps, session recordings, and user journey analysis, helping improve UX and site design. SEMrush, Ahrefs, and Moz specialize in SEO and competitive intelligence, enabling marketers to monitor keyword performance, backlinks, and search trends. Sprout Social, Hootsuite, and Brandwatch are key for social media analytics and audience engagement tracking. For conversion optimization and testing, tools like Optimizely, VWO, and Google Optimize support A/B testing and personalization. By integrating these tools into their analytics stack, marketers can gain a more complete, actionable view of performance across channels.

1. Google Tag Manager (GTM)

While Google Analytics is widely used, several other digital analytics tools offer complementary or specialized capabilities that enhance data-driven marketing. Adobe Analytics provides robust real-time data analysis and customization for enterprise-level needs. Hotjar and Microsoft Clarity offer visual behavior tracking through heatmaps, session recordings, and user journey analysis, helping improve UX and site design. SEMrush, Ahrefs, and Moz specialize in SEO and competitive intelligence, enabling marketers to monitor keyword performance, backlinks, and search trends. Sprout Social, Hootsuite, and Brandwatch are key for social media analytics and audience engagement tracking. For conversion optimization and testing, tools like Optimizely, VWO, and Google Optimize support A/B testing and personalization. By integrating these tools into their analytics stack, marketers can gain a more complete, actionable view of performance across channels.

- Tag management system to deploy tracking scripts without coding.
- Works with GA, Facebook Pixel, LinkedIn Insights, etc.

2. Google Data Studio (Looker Studio)

Google Data Studio, now known as Looker Studio, is a free and powerful data visualization tool that helps transform raw data into interactive and customizable dashboards and reports. It allows marketers and analysts to connect to various data sources such as Google Analytics, Google Ads,

BigQuery, Sheets, YouTube, and third-party platforms to create unified views of performance metrics. With its intuitive drag-and-drop interface, users can build dynamic charts, graphs, and tables without needing advanced technical skills. Looker Studio enables real-time data sharing and collaboration, making it easier to communicate insights across teams and stakeholders. Its flexibility and automation capabilities make it a valuable tool for monitoring KPIs, tracking campaign performance, and making data-driven decisions.

- Free dashboard and reporting tool.
- Visualizes data from GA, Google Ads, BigQuery, and third-party platforms.

3. Hotjar / Microsoft Clarity

Hotjar and Microsoft Clarity are user behavior analytics tools that provide visual insights into how visitors interact with your website. Both platforms offer heatmaps, session recordings, and click tracking, helping identify usability issues and optimize user experience. Hotjar is well-known for its additional features like surveys, feedback polls, and conversion funnels, making it ideal for gathering qualitative insights directly from users. Microsoft Clarity, on the other hand, is a free tool that excels in performance, scalability, and AI-driven insights like rage clicks and excessive scrolling. It also has no traffic limits and integrates easily with other Microsoft tools. Together, these tools help businesses better understand user behavior, reduce bounce rates, and increase conversions by turning interaction data into actionable improvements.

- Heatmaps, scroll maps, and session recordings.
- Helps visualize on-page user behavior.

4. SEMrush / Ahrefs / Moz

SEMrush, Ahrefs, and Moz are leading SEO and digital marketing tools that provide comprehensive insights into search engine performance, competitor strategies, and website optimization. SEMrush is known for its all-in-one capabilities, including keyword research, backlink analysis, site audits, PPC data, and content marketing tools, making it ideal for agencies and marketers managing multi-channel campaigns. Ahrefs excels in backlink analysis, boasting one of the largest link databases, and is favored for its in-depth site explorer, keyword tracking, and content gap analysis. Moz, with its user-friendly interface and tools like Domain Authority and Keyword Explorer, is popular among beginners and small businesses looking for accessible SEO solutions. Each platform offers unique strengths, and choosing the right one depends on your specific goals—whether it's technical SEO, competitor analysis, or content strategy.

- SEO analytics tools for keyword tracking, backlink analysis, and competitive insights.

5. HubSpot / Salesforce Marketing Cloud

HubSpot and Salesforce Marketing Cloud are powerful marketing automation platforms that support data-driven customer engagement across the entire buyer journey. HubSpot offers an all-in-one solution that includes CRM, email marketing, lead nurturing, social media management, and analytics. It's especially popular among small to mid-sized businesses for its ease of use, robust content marketing features, and seamless integration with sales and service tools. Salesforce Marketing Cloud, on the other hand, is geared toward enterprise-level organizations and excels in personalized, omnichannel campaign management. It offers advanced segmentation, AI-powered insights through Einstein, journey mapping, and deep integration with the broader Salesforce ecosystem. Both platforms provide powerful analytics and reporting capabilities, helping marketers optimize performance, boost ROI, and deliver highly targeted experiences based on real-time data.

- CRM platforms with built-in marketing and analytics features.
- Ideal for tracking user journeys from awareness to conversion.

6. Sprout Social / Hootsuite / Brandwatch

Sprout Social, Hootsuite, and Brandwatch are leading social media analytics and management tools, each offering distinct strengths for digital marketers. Sprout Social is known for its clean interface, powerful analytics, and excellent customer relationship management (CRM) features, making it ideal for teams focused on engagement and reporting. Hootsuite is one of the most widely used platforms for scheduling posts, monitoring multiple networks, and managing social content at scale—it's particularly popular for its broad integrations and affordability. Brandwatch, on the other hand, specializes in social listening and sentiment analysis, using AI to track brand mentions, consumer trends, and market insights across a vast range of digital channels. While Sprout and Hootsuite are ideal for content scheduling and performance reporting, Brandwatch excels in strategic monitoring and competitor intelligence, especially for larger organizations with a focus on brand perception.

- Social media analytics and listening tools.
- Measure engagement, monitor sentiment, and manage campaigns.

7. Adobe Analytics

Adobe Analytics is an advanced, enterprise-grade digital analytics platform designed for organizations seeking deep, customizable insights into user behavior across websites, apps, and other digital touchpoints. It goes beyond basic traffic tracking by enabling real-time data collection, multichannel attribution, and predictive analytics powered by Adobe Sensei (AI). With robust features like segmentation, cohort analysis, and flow visualization, Adobe Analytics allows businesses to uncover granular trends and optimize every stage of the customer journey. It also supports complex data integrations with other Adobe Experience Cloud tools, offering a unified view of marketing performance. While it requires more technical expertise and investment than tools like Google Analytics, its flexibility and depth make it a powerful solution for large organizations with sophisticated data needs.

- Enterprise-level analytics with advanced segmentation and predictive analysis.
- Highly customizable, ideal for large organizations.

8. Kissmetrics / Mixpanel

Kissmetrics and Mixpanel are advanced product and user analytics tools designed to help businesses understand how customers interact with their digital platforms over time. Kissmetrics is tailored for e-commerce and SaaS companies, offering deep insights into customer behavior, conversion funnels, and revenue attribution across the entire customer lifecycle. It emphasizes cohort analysis and customer segmentation, making it ideal for improving retention and lifetime value. Mixpanel, on the other hand, excels in event-based tracking and real-time data visualization, allowing product teams to analyze user flows, track feature adoption, and run A/B tests. With its intuitive interface and powerful funnel reports, Mixpanel is popular among product managers and growth teams aiming to build data-driven user experiences. Both platforms help turn behavioral data into actionable insights, but the right choice depends on whether your priority is marketing performance (Kissmetrics) or product engagement (Mixpanel).

- Funnel analysis and cohort tracking tools.
- Excellent for SaaS and product analytics.

7. Integrating Tools for a Holistic View

Integrating digital analytics tools is essential for creating a holistic view of marketing performance, customer behavior, and business impact. Since no single tool covers every aspect—from SEO and social media to user experience and sales—connecting platforms like Google Analytics, CRM systems (e.g., HubSpot or Salesforce), social media dashboards (e.g., Sprout Social), and user behavior tools (e.g., Hotjar or Mixpanel) provides a more complete and actionable picture. Integration enables centralized reporting, real-time data sharing, and deeper insights across the entire customer journey. By leveraging APIs, data connectors, and platforms like Looker Studio or BigQuery, marketers can break down silos, identify cross-channel trends, and align teams around unified KPIs. This interconnected ecosystem supports smarter decisions, more personalized customer experiences, and stronger ROI.

No single tool does everything. Smart marketers create a connected analytics stack:

- Use GA4 for traffic and behavior.
- Add GTM for flexible event tracking.
- Visualize in Looker Studio.
- Analyze user journeys with Hotjar.
- Track social sentiment with Brandwatch.
- Monitor ROI through Google Ads and CRM integration.

Example Stack:

- GA4 + GTM + Looker Studio + Hotjar + Google Ads + HubSpot

8. Data Privacy and Compliance

Data privacy and compliance are critical in digital analytics, as organizations must collect and use customer data responsibly and lawfully. Regulations such as the General Data Protection Regulation (GDPR) in the EU, California Consumer Privacy Act (CCPA) in the U.S., and other global frameworks set strict guidelines for transparency, consent, data storage, and user rights. Marketers must ensure that analytics tools are configured to respect user privacy—such as anonymizing IP addresses, managing cookie consent, and honoring opt-out preferences. Non-compliance can lead to legal penalties, reputational damage, and loss of customer trust. Prioritizing ethical data practices not only reduces risk but also builds long-term brand credibility and loyalty in an increasingly privacy-conscious landscape.

With increasing privacy regulations (GDPR, CCPA), analytics tools must:

- Offer IP anonymization.
- Allow data retention customization.
- Support user consent mechanisms.
- Use first-party cookies and server-side tagging when possible.

Conclusion

Analytics tools like Google Analytics empower marketers to measure what matters, optimize continuously, and drive meaningful business results. But GA is just the beginning — integrating multiple tools provides a richer, more actionable understanding of the digital ecosystem. Mastering these platforms is not just a technical skill — it's a strategic advantage.

CHAPTER THIRTEEN

Dashboards and Data Visualization

Introduction

In the data-driven world of digital marketing, having the right information is only half the battle — the other half is making that information clear, accessible, and actionable. This is where dashboards and data visualization play a crucial role. They translate complex data into visual stories that help stakeholders make faster, smarter decisions.

This chapter explores the importance of dashboards, principles of effective data visualization, commonly used tools, and real-world applications in marketing analytics.

1. What is a Dashboard?

A dashboard is a dynamic visual interface that consolidates and displays key performance indicators (KPIs), metrics, and critical data points in real time. It serves as a centralized hub where users can monitor performance across various digital channels, campaigns, or platforms—such as website traffic, conversion rates, social media engagement, and sales metrics. Dashboards help simplify complex data sets into digestible visualizations like charts, graphs, and tables, enabling faster insights and informed decision-making. Whether used for marketing, sales, or operations, dashboards enhance transparency, track progress toward goals, and support agile responses to changing business conditions.

Types of Dashboards:

- **Operational Dashboards:** Operational dashboards provide real-time data visualization designed for daily monitoring of key metrics and performance indicators. They offer teams instant access to up-to-date information, enabling quick detection of anomalies, progress tracking, and immediate response to any issues. By consolidating essential data in a clear, easy-to-read format, operational dashboards support efficient decision-making and keep everyone aligned on current business status. This continuous visibility is especially valuable for managing active campaigns, website performance, customer service, or sales operations, helping ensure smooth day-to-day functioning.

- **Strategic Dashboards:** Strategic dashboards focus on high-level metrics and key performance indicators that align closely with overall business goals and long-term objectives. Unlike operational dashboards, which emphasize real-time, day-to-day data, strategic dashboards provide a broader view of performance trends, progress toward goals, and insights that inform decision-making at the leadership level. They help executives and managers track critical areas such as revenue growth, market share, customer acquisition, and profitability, enabling strategic planning and resource allocation. By highlighting the big picture, strategic dashboards guide organizations in setting priorities, evaluating success, and steering future initiatives.

- **Analytical Dashboards:** Analytical dashboards are designed for in-depth exploration of data, enabling users to uncover patterns, trends, and insights that drive informed decision-making. These dashboards offer detailed, often customizable views that allow analysts and data teams to segment data, compare performance over time, and investigate underlying factors influencing results. By combining multiple data sources and interactive visualizations, analytical dashboards support complex analysis, hypothesis testing, and scenario modeling. They are essential for identifying opportunities, diagnosing problems, and optimizing strategies based on a thorough understanding of the data.

2. Importance of Dashboards in Marketing

Dashboards play a crucial role in marketing by providing real-time visibility into campaign performance, customer behavior, and key metrics across multiple channels. They help marketers quickly assess what's working and what needs adjustment, enabling data-driven decisions that improve ROI. By consolidating data from tools like Google Analytics, social media platforms, CRM systems, and ad networks, dashboards eliminate silos and offer a unified view of the marketing funnel. This not only saves time but also enhances collaboration among teams. Moreover, customizable dashboards can highlight specific KPIs aligned with business goals—such as lead generation, conversion rates, or engagement—making them essential for performance tracking, reporting, and strategic planning.

Dashboards empower marketing teams by:

- **Tracking Campaign Performance:** Tracking campaign performance involves monitoring key performance indicators (KPIs) such as click-through rate (CTR), cost per click (CPC), return on ad spend (ROAS), and bounce rates to evaluate how effectively your marketing efforts are driving results. CTR measures how many people click on your ads relative to impressions, indicating engagement. CPC tracks the cost efficiency of your paid campaigns. ROAS assesses the revenue generated compared to ad spend, showing overall profitability. Bounce rates reveal the percentage of visitors who leave after viewing only one page, highlighting potential issues with user experience or targeting. Regularly analyzing these KPIs helps optimize campaigns, improve budget allocation, and maximize ROI.
- **Identifying Trends Quickly:** Identifying trends quickly means being able to detect emerging patterns, shifts in user behavior, or market changes as they happen, enabling you to seize opportunities or address problems before they escalate. Real-time data monitoring and alert systems help marketers stay agile, responding swiftly to spikes in demand, sudden drops in engagement, or competitor moves. Early trend detection supports proactive decision-making, allowing for timely campaign adjustments, resource reallocation, or crisis management. This agility can provide a significant competitive advantage by keeping your

strategies aligned with evolving audience needs and market conditions.

- **Improving Communication:** Improving communication involves effectively sharing performance data and insights with teams, clients, and executives in a clear, concise, and tailored manner. By using well-designed reports, dashboards, and presentations, you ensure that each audience understands key metrics relevant to their role and interests. Transparent communication fosters alignment, encourages collaboration, and builds trust by demonstrating accountability and progress toward goals. Additionally, sharing insights regularly helps stakeholders make informed decisions, set realistic expectations, and support ongoing optimization efforts—ultimately driving better results across the organization.

- **Saving Time:** Saving time by automating reports means setting up tools and systems that generate and deliver performance data automatically, eliminating the need for manual data collection and formatting. Automation ensures reports are consistently accurate, timely, and easy to access, freeing up valuable time for teams to focus on analysis and strategy rather than repetitive tasks. This efficiency reduces human error, speeds up decision-making, and allows for more frequent monitoring, helping businesses stay agile and responsive to changing conditions without the burden of manual reporting processes.

- **Enhancing Decision-Making:** Enhancing decision-making means grounding your marketing and business strategies in real, data-driven insights rather than assumptions or guesswork. By analyzing accurate and relevant data, you gain a clear understanding of customer behavior, campaign performance, and market trends, which helps you make informed choices that are more likely to succeed. This approach reduces risks, uncovers opportunities, and ensures resources are allocated effectively. Ultimately, decisions based on solid insights lead to smarter strategies, better outcomes, and a stronger competitive advantage.

3. What is Data Visualization?

Data visualization is the process of representing data and information through graphical elements such as charts, graphs, maps, and infographics. It transforms raw, complex data sets into visual formats that are easier to understand, interpret, and act upon. By highlighting trends, patterns, and outliers, data visualization helps stakeholders quickly grasp insights that might be missed in spreadsheets or text-based reports. It plays a vital role in decision-making, storytelling, and communicating performance across teams—especially in fields like marketing, finance, and operations. Effective visualizations not only make data more accessible but also drive engagement and clarity in strategic discussions.

Common Visualization Types:

- **Bar and Column Charts:** Bar and column charts are ideal for comparing categories because they visually display data as rectangular bars—horizontal for bar charts and vertical for column charts—making it easy to see differences in size or value across groups. These charts clearly highlight comparisons between discrete categories, such as sales by region, website traffic sources, or campaign performance metrics. Their straightforward layout helps audiences quickly grasp relative performance and trends, making them a popular choice for presenting categorical data in reports and dashboards.

- **Line Charts:** Line charts are perfect for showing trends over time because they connect data points with a continuous line, making it easy to visualize changes, patterns, and fluctuations across a timeline. Whether tracking monthly sales, daily website visits, or campaign performance over weeks, line charts help reveal upward or downward trends, seasonality, and anomalies. Their clear, flowing design allows viewers to quickly understand how metrics evolve, making them a valuable tool for monitoring progress and informing strategic decisions.

- **Pie and Donut Charts:** Pie and donut charts are great for illustrating composition and distribution because they visually represent parts of a whole as slices of a circle. Each slice shows the proportion or percentage of a category relative to the total, making it easy to understand how different segments contribute to the overall picture. While pie charts display the full circle, donut charts have a hollow center, which can be used to add additional context or labels. These charts are especially useful for showing market share, traffic sources, or budget allocation, helping audiences quickly grasp the relative size of each component.

- **Heatmaps:** Heatmaps are visual tools that display data intensity or frequency using color gradients, making them perfect for showing where users focus their attention—such as clicks, scrolls, or mouse movements on web pages. Areas with higher activity appear in warmer colors (like red or orange), while less active spots show cooler tones (like blue or green). Heatmaps help identify popular content, usability issues, or navigation patterns, enabling marketers and designers to optimize site layout and user experience by focusing on the most engaging or problematic areas.

- **Scatter Plots:** Scatter plots are used to visualize relationships and correlations between two variables by plotting individual data points on a two-dimensional graph. Each point represents a pair of values, allowing you to see patterns, trends, or clusters that indicate how one variable may affect or relate to the other. Scatter plots are especially useful for identifying positive or negative correlations, outliers, and data distribution, helping analysts uncover insights that inform strategy and decision-making.

- **Funnel Charts:** Funnel charts are ideal for visualizing conversion paths or sales pipelines because they show the progressive reduction of data as users move through different stages. Each section of the funnel represents a step—such as website visits, leads, qualified prospects, and final sales—with the width shrinking to reflect drop-off rates. This format makes it easy to identify where potential customers are lost, highlight bottlenecks, and prioritize areas for improvement. Funnel charts help businesses optimize the customer journey and increase conversion rates by providing clear, stage-by-stage insights.

- **Gauge Charts:** Gauge charts are effective for displaying KPIs with specific targets—like revenue against a goal—by visually representing progress on a dial or meter. The needle points to the current value within a range, showing at a glance whether performance is below, meeting, or exceeding expectations. This intuitive format makes it easy for stakeholders to quickly assess how close you are to hitting critical benchmarks, making gauge charts especially useful in dashboards for tracking goals, quotas, or service levels in a clear and motivating way.

4. Key Principles of Effective Visualization

Effective data visualization is guided by key principles that ensure clarity, accuracy, and impact. First, simplicity is essential—visuals should focus on the message without unnecessary complexity or clutter. Clarity ensures that data is easy to read and interpret, using appropriate chart types, scales, and labels. Accuracy is critical; visuals must represent data truthfully without distortion or manipulation. Context adds meaning—providing benchmarks, timeframes, or comparisons that help users understand what the data implies. Lastly, visual hierarchy helps guide the viewer's attention, using layout, color, and emphasis to prioritize key insights. When these principles are applied, visualizations become powerful tools for storytelling, decision-making, and data communication.

To make visual data intuitive and insightful:

Principle	Description
Clarity	Avoid clutter; highlight what matters most.
Context	Add labels, titles, and time ranges for understanding.
Consistency	Use uniform colors, units, and formats.
Comparability	Allow users to compare performance across periods or campaigns.
Interactivity	Enable filtering and drill-downs where possible.
Storytelling	Guide viewers through data narratives rather than dumping numbers.

5. Tools for Dashboards and Data Visualization

A wide range of tools are available for creating dashboards and data visualizations, each tailored to different user needs, skill levels, and business goals. Looker Studio (formerly Google Data Studio) is a popular free option for building interactive dashboards with seamless integration into Google's ecosystem. Tableau is renowned for its powerful visualization capabilities and is ideal for users who need advanced analytics and custom visuals. Power BI, from Microsoft, offers strong business intelligence features and integrates well with Office 365 and Azure. Domo, Qlik Sense, and Sisense provide enterprise-grade dashboard solutions with scalable architecture and real-time data processing. For marketers and product teams, tools like Klipfolio, Geckoboard, and Chartio offer intuitive interfaces and quick connectivity to marketing platforms, CRMs, and databases. Choosing the right tool depends on factors like budget, data complexity, integration needs, and the level of interactivity required.

1. Google Looker Studio (formerly Data Studio)

Google Looker Studio, formerly known as Google Data Studio, is a free and user-friendly tool for building interactive dashboards and visual reports. It allows users to connect and unify data from multiple sources—including Google Analytics, Google Ads, Google Sheets, BigQuery, and various third-party platforms—into a single, customizable interface.

With its intuitive drag-and-drop design, Looker Studio makes it easy to create dynamic charts, tables, and graphs without requiring coding expertise. Users can share dashboards in real time, collaborate across teams, and automate reporting workflows. Its flexibility, real-time connectivity, and seamless integration with Google's ecosystem make it a powerful choice for marketers, analysts, and business teams seeking to visualize performance and drive informed decisions.

- Free, user-friendly dashboard tool.
- Integrates with Google Analytics, Ads, Sheets, and other sources.
- Customizable with real-time data.

2. Microsoft Power BI

Microsoft Power BI is a powerful business analytics and data visualization tool designed to help organizations turn raw data into actionable insights. It enables users to create interactive dashboards, reports, and data models by connecting to a wide range of data sources—including Excel, SQL databases, cloud services, and third-party platforms. Power BI integrates seamlessly with other Microsoft products like Excel, Azure, and Teams, making it especially valuable for businesses already within the Microsoft ecosystem. Its advanced features, such as AI-powered insights, natural language queries, and real-time data streaming, support both technical and non-technical users in uncovering trends, forecasting outcomes, and making data-driven decisions. With scalable capabilities for individual users to large enterprises, Power BI is a go-to solution for robust, enterprise-grade reporting and visualization.

- Enterprise-level BI tool with powerful visualization and data modeling.
- Connects to a wide range of data sources.

3. Tableau

Tableau is a leading data visualization and business intelligence platform known for its ability to transform complex data into clear, interactive, and visually compelling dashboards. Designed for both analysts and business users, Tableau supports connections to hundreds of data sources, including spreadsheets, databases, cloud services, and big data platforms. Its intuitive drag-and-drop interface, coupled with advanced capabilities like real-time analytics, forecasting, and geospatial mapping, allows users to uncover insights and tell data-driven stories with ease. Tableau also offers Tableau Public for sharing visualizations publicly and Tableau Server/Cloud for secure collaboration across teams. With strong community support and extensive customization options, Tableau is ideal for organizations seeking in-depth analytics, rich visual exploration, and scalable deployment across departments.

- Popular for interactive dashboards and visual storytelling.
- Great for large-scale data sets and deep analytics.

4. Excel / Google Sheets

Excel and Google Sheets remain foundational tools for data analysis and visualization, offering flexibility, accessibility, and broad functionality for users of all skill levels. Microsoft Excel is known for its advanced features such as pivot tables, complex formulas, VBA scripting, and add-ins like Power Query and Power Pivot, making it ideal for in-depth data manipulation and financial modeling. Google Sheets, on the other hand, shines with its cloud-based collaboration, real-time editing, and easy integration with other Google Workspace apps. Both tools support basic charting and dashboard creation, making them suitable for lightweight reporting, quick analyses, or prototyping before moving to more sophisticated platforms like Power BI or Tableau. Their widespread use and familiarity make them indispensable in both small businesses and enterprise environments.

- Useful for quick charts and basic dashboards.
- Best for small-scale or static reports.

5. Klipfolio, Databox, Datorama

Klipfolio, Databox, and Datorama are cloud-based dashboard and data visualization platforms designed to help businesses monitor performance across multiple tools and data sources. Klipfolio is known for its customizable dashboards, real-time data updates, and wide range of integrations with marketing, sales, and analytics platforms—ideal for data-savvy teams that want granular control over visualizations. Databox offers an intuitive, mobile-friendly interface with pre-built templates and goal tracking, making it especially appealing for marketing teams that need quick, visually appealing reports without technical complexity. Datorama, a Salesforce product, is tailored for enterprise marketers and excels in unifying disparate marketing data through AI-powered insights, deep integrations, and cross-channel analytics. While Klipfolio and Databox are great for small to mid-sized businesses, Datorama is suited for larger organizations seeking a unified marketing intelligence platform.

- Specialized marketing dashboard tools.
- Focused on connecting multiple marketing platforms.

6. Supermetrics

Connector tool that extracts data from platforms (Facebook, Instagram, LinkedIn, etc.) into Sheets or dashboards. Supermetrics is a powerful data integration tool designed to simplify the process of collecting and transferring marketing data into platforms like Google Sheets, Excel, Looker Studio, Power BI, and BigQuery. It connects with a wide range of marketing sources—such as Google Analytics, Facebook Ads, LinkedIn, HubSpot, and many others—allowing users to automate reporting, consolidate data, and eliminate manual copy-pasting. Supermetrics is especially valuable for marketers and analysts who want to build custom dashboards or perform deeper analysis without needing to write complex code or queries. Its scheduling and refresh features ensure data stays up to date, while its plug-and-play connectors make it easy to scale across teams. Whether for campaign tracking, performance comparison, or ROI analysis, Supermetrics boosts efficiency and enhances the value of your data ecosystem.

6. Common Marketing Dashboard Examples

Common marketing dashboards serve different strategic purposes, helping teams track, analyze, and optimize various aspects of their campaigns. A campaign performance dashboard shows key metrics like impressions, clicks, CTR, and conversions across channels (Google Ads, Facebook, LinkedIn). A social media dashboard monitors engagement, follower growth, reach, and sentiment across platforms like Instagram, Twitter, and LinkedIn. For inbound marketing, a content performance dashboard tracks blog views, bounce rates, time on page, and lead conversions. Email marketing dashboards measure open rates, click-throughs, unsubscribe rates, and A/B test results. Meanwhile, SEO dashboards display organic traffic, keyword rankings, backlink performance, and technical site health. These dashboards not only visualize real-time performance but also help identify trends, assess ROI, and inform data-driven decision-making across marketing functions.

1. Website Performance Dashboard

A Website Performance Dashboard provides a comprehensive view of how well a website is functioning in terms of user experience, traffic, and conversion. It typically includes key metrics such as page views, unique visitors, bounce rate, average session duration, and pages per session. For deeper insights, it may also track traffic sources (organic, paid, referral, direct), top-performing landing pages, exit rates, and goal completions like form submissions or purchases. Tools like Google Analytics, Looker Studio, and Hotjar often power these dashboards, enabling marketers and web teams to identify usability issues, optimize content and navigation, and measure the impact of SEO and advertising efforts. By visualizing this data in real time, a website performance dashboard supports ongoing optimization and a better user experience.

- Users, sessions, bounce rate, average session duration.
- Top landing pages and traffic sources.

2. Social Media Dashboard

A Social Media Dashboard centralizes performance metrics across various platforms—such as Facebook, Instagram, Twitter, LinkedIn, and TikTok—allowing marketers to track engagement, audience growth, and content effectiveness in one place. Common metrics include follower count, likes, shares, comments, reach, impressions, click-through rates, and engagement rate. Advanced dashboards may also include sentiment analysis, influencer performance, hashtag tracking, and post-level breakdowns to identify high-performing content. Tools like Sprout Social, Hootsuite, Buffer, and Looker Studio (with social connectors) make it easy to visualize and analyze social KPIs. A well-designed social media dashboard helps teams monitor campaign success, compare channel performance, schedule content more effectively, and make data-driven decisions for improving brand presence and audience engagement.

- Followers, engagement rate, post reach, impressions.
- Best-performing posts or content types.

3. SEO Dashboard

An SEO Dashboard provides a centralized view of search engine optimization performance, helping marketers and SEO specialists monitor visibility, traffic, and technical health. Key metrics typically include organic traffic, keyword rankings, click-through rate (CTR) from search results, bounce rate, backlink profile, and domain authority. It may also display top-performing pages, indexing issues, site speed, crawl errors, and mobile usability—often sourced from tools like Google Search Console, Google Analytics, SEMrush, Ahrefs, or Moz. An effective SEO dashboard helps identify content opportunities, track the impact of optimization efforts, and diagnose technical problems that affect rankings. By surfacing these insights in real time, it enables faster, more informed decision-making to improve search visibility and organic growth.

- Organic traffic, keyword rankings, backlinks, crawl errors.

4. Paid Ads Dashboard

A Paid Ads Dashboard consolidates performance data from advertising platforms like Google Ads, Facebook Ads, LinkedIn Ads, and Twitter Ads, providing marketers with a real-time view of campaign effectiveness. Key metrics typically include impressions, clicks, click-through rate (CTR), cost-per-click (CPC), conversion rate, cost-per-conversion (CPA), return on ad spend (ROAS), and total spend. Advanced dashboards may also segment data by audience, location, device, or campaign type to uncover deeper insights. Tools such as Looker Studio, Supermetrics, Databox, and Datorama can automate data pulls and visualize results across platforms. This type of dashboard helps marketers optimize ad performance, allocate budgets more effectively, identify underperforming assets, and align paid strategies with broader business goals.

- Impressions, CTR, CPC, conversion rate, ROAS by channel.

5. Email Marketing Dashboard

A Paid Ads Dashboard consolidates performance data from advertising platforms like Google Ads, Facebook Ads, LinkedIn Ads, and Twitter Ads, providing marketers with a real-time view of campaign effectiveness. Key metrics typically include impressions, clicks, click-through rate (CTR), cost-per-click (CPC), conversion rate, cost-per-conversion (CPA), return on ad spend (ROAS), and total spend. Advanced dashboards may also segment data by audience, location, device, or campaign type to uncover deeper insights. Tools such as Looker Studio, Supermetrics, Databox, and Datorama can automate data pulls and visualize results across platforms. This type of dashboard helps marketers optimize ad performance, allocate budgets more effectively, identify underperforming assets, and align paid strategies with broader business goals.

- Open rate, click rate, unsubscribe rate, campaign comparisons.

7. How to Build an Effective Dashboard

Building an effective dashboard starts with clearly defining its purpose and audience—whether it's for executives tracking KPIs, marketers monitoring campaign performance, or analysts exploring trends. Next, identify the key metrics that align with business goals, ensuring they are measurable, relevant, and actionable. Choose the right tools based on your data sources and visualization needs (e.g., Looker Studio, Power BI, Tableau). Then, connect your data sources—such as Google Analytics, CRM platforms, or ad networks—and ensure the data is clean and up to date. When designing the dashboard, prioritize simplicity and clarity: use consistent formats, intuitive layouts, and visual hierarchy to highlight important insights. Incorporate filters or interactive elements for deeper analysis, and make sure the dashboard is regularly updated and shared with stakeholders. Finally, test usability and gather feedback to continuously refine its effectiveness.

- **Define Your Audience:** The primary users of Digital Marketing Analytics are executives, marketers, and clients. Executives use the analytics to monitor overall business performance, track key metrics, and guide strategic decisions. Marketers rely on detailed data insights to optimize campaigns, understand audience behavior, and improve marketing effectiveness. Clients use the analytics to evaluate the success of marketing efforts and justify investments by seeing clear, actionable results. Understanding these distinct user groups helps tailor the analytics tools and reports to meet their specific needs and goals.
- **Choose the Right KPIs:** Choosing the right KPIs means aligning your metrics directly with your business and marketing objectives rather than focusing on vanity metrics that look good but don't drive meaningful results. For example, instead of just tracking website visits or social

media likes, focus on KPIs like conversion rates, customer acquisition cost, lifetime value, or return on ad spend. These actionable metrics provide real insight into performance and help guide strategic decisions to achieve your goals effectively.

- **Connect Data Sources:** Connecting data sources is crucial to achieving real-time accuracy in digital marketing analytics. By integrating various platforms—such as social media, CRM systems, email marketing tools, and web analytics—into a unified dashboard, you ensure that data flows seamlessly and updates instantly. This real-time connection allows marketers and decision-makers to monitor campaign performance live, quickly identify trends or issues, and make timely, informed adjustments to optimize results. Without synchronized data sources, insights risk being outdated or incomplete, reducing the effectiveness of marketing strategies.

- **Design for Clarity:** Designing for clarity is essential in digital marketing analytics to ensure insights are easily understood and actionable. Use colors strategically to highlight key metrics—such as green for positive trends and red for alerts—while avoiding overwhelming or distracting palettes. Organize information with a clear layout that guides the viewer's eye, placing the most important data at the top or center. Employ visual hierarchy through font size, bolding, and spacing to differentiate headings, subheadings, and data points. This thoughtful design approach helps users quickly grasp insights, reducing confusion and enabling faster, smarter decision-making.

- **Test and Iterate:** Testing and iterating are vital steps to ensure digital marketing analytics remain user-friendly and relevant. By gathering feedback from actual users—whether executives, marketers, or clients—you can identify pain points, unclear data presentations, or missing insights. Use this input to refine the user experience (UX), improve dashboard navigation, and adjust which data points are highlighted to better align with users' goals. Continuous iteration helps keep the analytics tools adaptable to changing business needs, ensuring they deliver meaningful, actionable insights that drive ongoing improvement.

8. Real-World Example

A real-world example of dashboard effectiveness can be seen in how a mid-sized e-commerce company used a combined marketing performance dashboard to improve ROI. Using Looker Studio integrated with Google Analytics, Facebook Ads, Mailchimp, and Shopify, the company built a real-time dashboard that tracked key metrics such as traffic sources, conversion rates, customer acquisition cost (CAC), and email open rates. By visualizing cross-channel data in one place, the marketing team quickly identified that while paid ads were generating high traffic, most conversions were coming from organic search and email campaigns. This insight prompted a budget shift toward content marketing and automation, leading to a 15% increase in overall ROI within three months. The dashboard not only streamlined reporting but also became a strategic decision-making tool for campaign planning and resource allocation.

Example: E-commerce Digital Dashboard

An E-commerce Digital Dashboard is designed to give online retailers a comprehensive view of their digital sales performance, customer behavior, and marketing efficiency. It typically includes core KPIs such as total sales, average order value (AOV), conversion rate, cart abandonment rate, and customer lifetime value (CLV). It also tracks website traffic sources, campaign performance (e.g., from Google Ads, Facebook Ads), and email engagement metrics. Platforms like Shopify, Google Analytics, and Klaviyo can be integrated using tools like Looker Studio, Power BI, or Supermetrics to visualize these insights in real time. For deeper analysis, the dashboard might segment data by product category, device, or location, helping teams identify top-selling products, high-performing channels, and bottlenecks in the purchase journey. This holistic view enables data-driven decisions to improve user experience, increase sales, and optimize marketing spend.

An e-commerce company uses Google Looker Studio to combine:

An e-commerce company uses Google Looker Studio to combine data from multiple sources—such as Google Analytics 4 for website traffic and user behavior, Shopify for sales and product data, Google Ads for paid campaign performance, and Klaviyo for email marketing metrics—into a unified, interactive dashboard. This integration allows the marketing and sales teams to monitor real-time performance across the customer journey, from ad impressions to completed purchases. Key metrics displayed include traffic sources, conversion rates, return on ad spend (ROAS), top-selling products, and email open/click rates. With Looker Studio's customizable filters and visualizations, the company can segment data by device, region, or channel, identify trends, and quickly respond to performance shifts. This streamlined view supports faster decision-making, more effective budget allocation, and a more personalized customer experience.

- Google Analytics (site behavior)
- Shopify data (sales)
- Facebook Ads (spend and ROAS)
- Email (Klaviyo or Mailchimp engagement)

This dashboard gives real-time visibility into marketing ROI, top-performing campaigns, customer retention, and checkout behavior — all in one place.

Conclusion

Dashboards and data visualization turn raw metrics into meaningful insights. By designing clear, interactive, and goal-focused visual interfaces, marketers can not only track performance but also communicate value, align teams, and drive smarter decisions. As data grows more abundant, the ability to visualize it effectively becomes a superpower in the marketer's toolkit.

CHAPTER FOURTEEN

Attribution Modeling and Multi-Touch Analysis

Introduction

In today's fragmented digital landscape, a customer's journey to purchase often spans multiple channels, devices, and touchpoints. Relying solely on last-click attribution hides the true drivers of performance. To optimize marketing efforts and allocate budget effectively, marketers must embrace attribution modeling and multi-touch analysis.

This chapter explores the principles of attribution, different modeling techniques, the benefits of multi-touch analysis, and how businesses can apply these strategies for more accurate performance evaluation.

1. What is Attribution in Marketing?

Attribution in marketing refers to the process of identifying which marketing touchpoints or channels contribute to a conversion or desired customer action, such as a sale, sign-up, or download. It helps marketers understand the customer journey and determine how different campaigns, ads, emails, or social media interactions influence buying behavior. By assigning credit to specific channels or steps—like a Google ad click, an email open, or a blog visit—attribution models reveal what's working and what isn't. This insight is crucial for optimizing budget allocation, improving campaign strategies, and maximizing return on investment (ROI). Accurate attribution enables data-driven decisions by showing not just what led to a conversion, but how and when various touchpoints played a role in driving it.

Attribution is the process of assigning credit to various marketing touchpoints that contribute to a desired outcome (e.g., purchase, lead, download). It answers the question:

"Which channels and campaigns truly drive conversions?"

2. Types of Attribution Models

Attribution models determine how credit for a conversion is assigned across the customer journey. There are several attribution models used in marketing to assign credit to touchpoints along the customer journey, each offering a different perspective. First-click attribution gives 100% credit to the first interaction a customer had with a brand, emphasizing initial awareness. In contrast, last-click attribution credits the final interaction before conversion, focusing on the moment of decision. Linear attribution distributes credit equally across all touchpoints, highlighting the collective impact of each step. Time-decay attribution gives more weight to interactions that occurred closer to the conversion, recognizing their increasing influence. Position-based (U-shaped) attribution assigns more credit to the first and last interactions, with less weight to the middle steps. Advanced approaches like data-driven attribution use machine learning to analyze the actual impact of each touchpoint based on historical data. Choosing the right model depends on campaign goals, sales cycle length, and the complexity of the customer journey.

A. Single-Touch Models

Single-touch attribution models assign 100% of the conversion credit to just one touchpoint in the customer journey, making them simple to implement but limited in insight. The two most common types are First-

Touch Attribution, which gives full credit to the first interaction (useful for measuring awareness campaigns), and Last-Touch Attribution, which credits the final interaction before conversion (often used to evaluate direct-response efforts). While easy to understand and implement, these models ignore the influence of intermediate touchpoints and may oversimplify complex, multi-channel journeys. Single-touch models are best suited for short sales cycles or when you want to emphasize either acquisition or closing efforts, but they fall short in capturing the full path to conversion in more nuanced marketing ecosystems.

Credit is given to one touchpoint only.

Model	Description
First-Touch	All credit goes to the first interaction.
Last-Touch	All credit goes to the last interaction.
Last Non-Direct Click	Skips direct visits, credits last indirect.

Limitation: Oversimplifies the journey; ignores all but one touchpoint.

B. Multi-Touch Attribution (MTA) Models

Multi-Touch Attribution (MTA) models distribute credit for a conversion across multiple touchpoints in the customer journey, offering a more balanced and realistic view of how various channels and interactions contribute to success. Unlike single-touch models, MTA acknowledges that customers often engage with a brand several times before converting. Common MTA models include Linear Attribution, which gives equal credit to each touchpoint; Time-Decay Attribution, which gives more weight to interactions closer to the conversion; and Position-Based (U-Shaped), which emphasizes the first and last interactions while assigning lesser credit to the middle ones. More advanced is Data-Driven Attribution, which uses machine learning to assign credit based on each channel's actual impact, derived from historical data patterns. MTA helps marketers understand how different strategies work together, optimize channel mix, and improve return on investment across complex, multi-channel campaigns.

Credit is distributed across multiple touchpoints.

Model	Description
Linear	Equal credit to all touchpoints.
Time Decay	More credit to recent interactions.
Position-Based (U-Shaped)	40% to first, 40% to last, 20% split among the rest.
W-Shaped	Equal credit to first, lead conversion, and last touch (typically 30% each).
Custom / Algorithmic	Data-driven models using machine learning to assign value based on behavior and outcomes.

3. The Need for Multi-Touch Analysis

Multi-touch analysis is essential in today's digital marketing landscape because customer journeys are rarely linear and often involve multiple interactions across different channels before a conversion occurs. Relying on single-touch attribution oversimplifies this journey and can lead to misguided budget allocation or missed optimization opportunities. Multi-touch analysis provides a more comprehensive view by evaluating the cumulative impact of various touchpoints—such as a social media ad, email campaign, website visit, and Google search—throughout the decision-making process. This allows marketers to understand which combinations of interactions are most effective, identify high-performing channels, and refine strategies accordingly. By using data from multi-touch models, businesses can make smarter, data-driven decisions, optimize spend across the funnel, and ultimately improve both conversion rates and return on investment (ROI).

Customer journeys are rarely linear. A person might:

See a Facebook ad → Google your brand → Visit website → Leave → Return via email → Convert after a YouTube remarketing ad.

Multi-Touch Analysis (MTA) captures the *full* path and allocates value based on the contribution of each step.

Benefits of MTA:

- Clearer understanding of complex user journeys.
- Improved ROI measurement by recognizing assistive channels.
- Smarter budget allocation based on true influence.
- Enhanced personalization by identifying key drivers of conversion.

4. Tools for Attribution and Multi-Touch Analysis

Several tools help marketers perform attribution and multi-touch analysis, each offering different capabilities depending on campaign complexity, data sources, and business goals. Google Analytics 4 (GA4) provides built-in attribution reports and supports data-driven models, ideal for understanding cross-channel journeys. Adobe Analytics offers robust, customizable attribution and segmentation features for enterprise-level insights. HubSpot and Salesforce Marketing Cloud include integrated attribution tracking tied to CRM data, making them powerful for B2B and lead nurturing. Wicked Reports and Triple Whale are tailored for e-commerce, focusing on revenue attribution and customer lifetime value. Rockerbox and Segment help unify touchpoint data from multiple platforms for more accurate multi-touch insights. Many of these tools integrate with Looker Studio, Power BI, or Tableau to create interactive dashboards that visualize attribution results, helping teams optimize marketing performance across the full customer journey.

Tool / Platform	Key Features
Google Analytics 4	Event-based tracking; supports multiple attribution models and comparisons.
Google Ads	Conversion paths, attribution reports, and model comparison tools.
Meta Ads Manager	Attribution settings for cross-device and multi-channel ads.
HubSpot / Salesforce	CRM-integrated multi-touch attribution for lead gen and sales pipelines.
Adobe Analytics	Advanced attribution modeling and customizable rules-based models.
Wicked Reports / Triple Whale / Ruler Analytics	Purpose-built tools for e-commerce and performance attribution.

5. Comparing Attribution Models: Practical Example

Imagine a customer sees a Facebook ad, then reads a blog post, later clicks on a Google Search ad, and finally signs up through an email campaign. Using First-Touch Attribution, all credit would go to the Facebook ad, while Last-Touch Attribution would credit the email. A Linear Attribution model would split credit equally across all four touchpoints

(25% each), whereas a Time-Decay model would give more credit to the email and Google ad, since they occurred closer to the conversion. A Position-Based model (e.g., 40-20-40) might assign 40% to the Facebook ad and email, and 20% shared between the blog and Google ad. Finally, Data-Driven Attribution would use historical data and machine learning to determine the actual impact of each step, which might show the blog had more influence than initially assumed. This comparison shows how model choice affects performance insights—and ultimately, budget and strategy decisions.

Let's say a customer takes the following path:

1. Clicks on a Facebook ad
2. Visits website via Google organic search
3. Clicks on an email campaign
4. Converts after a Google search ad

Model	Attribution Breakdown
Last Click	100% to Google search ad
First Click	100% to Facebook ad
Linear	25% to each touchpoint
Time Decay	Most credit to Google search ad, less to earlier ones
Position-Based	40% to Facebook (first), 40% to Google search ad (last), 20% split between others

6. Attribution Challenges

Despite its value, marketing attribution comes with several challenges that can impact accuracy and decision-making. One major issue is data fragmentation—customer interactions often span multiple platforms (web, mobile, in-store), and not all tools integrate seamlessly, leading to incomplete visibility. Cross-device tracking is another hurdle, as users may switch between smartphones, laptops, and tablets, making it difficult to connect all touchpoints to a single user journey. Privacy regulations like GDPR and the phasing out of third-party cookies further limit tracking capabilities, reducing the granularity of available data. Additionally, choosing the wrong attribution model can lead to misleading conclusions, such as overvaluing last-click performance while ignoring important upper-funnel activities. Lastly, organizational silos between marketing, sales, and analytics teams can hinder alignment and data sharing, making it difficult to implement accurate, consistent attribution across the business.

- **Cross-Device Tracking:** Cross-device tracking is essential because users frequently switch between phones, laptops, tablets, and other devices throughout their customer journey. Implementing robust cross-device tracking enables marketers to accurately attribute actions and understand user behavior across all touchpoints, providing a complete, unified view of the customer. This insight helps optimize campaigns, personalize messaging, and improve conversion rates by ensuring that interactions on any device contribute to the overall analytics and strategy. Without it, data can be fragmented, leading to incomplete or misleading conclusions.

- **Data Silos:** Data silos occur when different platforms—like Facebook Ads and Google Analytics—don't seamlessly share or integrate data, leading to fragmented and inconsistent insights. This lack of data harmonization can create challenges in getting a complete, accurate picture of marketing performance, as each system may report metrics differently or track user actions in isolation. Overcoming data silos requires implementing integration tools, standardized tracking methods, or data warehouses to consolidate and reconcile information, enabling marketers to make better-informed decisions based on unified, comprehensive data.

- **Offline Conversions:** Offline conversions, such as in-store visits or phone calls, present a challenge because they're often difficult to directly link to digital marketing efforts. Without connecting these offline actions to online touchpoints, it's hard to measure the true impact of campaigns on real-world customer behavior. To bridge this gap, marketers can use strategies like unique promo codes, call tracking numbers, or loyalty programs, alongside CRM integrations, to capture and attribute offline conversions back to specific digital interactions. This comprehensive tracking helps create a fuller picture of customer journeys and campaign effectiveness.

- **Privacy Regulations:** Privacy regulations like GDPR and CCPA significantly impact digital marketing analytics by restricting how user data can be collected, stored, and shared. These laws require transparency, user consent, and data protection, limiting the ability to track individuals across websites and devices without explicit permission. As a result, marketers must adapt by implementing privacy-compliant tracking methods, such as anonymized data collection, first-party cookies, and consent management tools. Navigating these regulations carefully ensures legal compliance while still gaining valuable insights to optimize marketing strategies.

- **Model Bias:** Model bias occurs when attribution or analytics models unintentionally favor certain marketing channels over others because of their design or underlying assumptions. For example, last-click models might overvalue the final touchpoint, while neglecting earlier interactions that influenced the customer journey. This bias can skew decision-making, leading to misallocated budgets or overlooked opportunities. To minimize model bias, it's important to use a combination of attribution models, regularly review their performance, and incorporate data-driven or multi-touch approaches that more accurately reflect the true impact of each channel.

7. Best Practices for Effective Attribution

To ensure accurate and actionable attribution, marketers should follow a set of best practices. Start by defining clear goals—know what you want to measure (e.g., conversions, sales, sign-ups) and why. Use multi-touch attribution models when possible to capture the full customer journey, rather than relying solely on first- or last-touch models. Ensure data quality and consistency by integrating reliable, unified data sources across platforms (web, CRM, email, ads, etc.). Choose an attribution tool that matches your business size and marketing complexity, and test different models to see which provides the most meaningful insights. Regularly validate your attribution logic against real-world outcomes, and involve cross-functional teams (marketing, sales, analytics) to interpret results collaboratively. Finally, always consider privacy compliance, using transparent, consent-based tracking to maintain data integrity and customer trust.

1. **Use GA4's Attribution Reports:** Using GA4's Attribution Reports allows marketers to compare the outcomes of different attribution models—such as last-click, first-click, and data-driven attribution—within one platform. This comparison helps reveal how

credit is assigned to various marketing channels across the customer journey, providing deeper insights into which touchpoints drive conversions. By analyzing these differences, marketers can make more informed decisions on budget allocation, optimize campaigns for better performance, and reduce the risk of model bias affecting their strategies. GA4's flexible reports make it easier to understand and act on attribution data effectively.

2. **Integrate CRM and Ad Platforms:** Integrating CRM systems with ad platforms bridges the gap between online behavior and actual sales outcomes. By linking customer data from ads with CRM records—such as leads, opportunities, and closed deals—marketers gain a clear view of how digital campaigns translate into real revenue. This integration enables better tracking of the full customer journey, more precise attribution, and improved targeting based on customer profiles and purchase history. Ultimately, it helps optimize marketing spend and drives strategies that directly impact business growth.

3. **Choose Models Based on Goals:**

   - **Awareness campaigns:** For awareness campaigns, using a first-touch attribution model can be particularly useful because it gives full credit to the initial interaction that introduced a potential customer to your brand. Since the goal of awareness campaigns is to capture attention and start the customer journey, understanding which channels or ads generate that first engagement helps optimize where to invest for maximum reach and brand exposure. First-touch attribution highlights the effectiveness of top-of-funnel efforts, guiding marketers to refine messaging and placements that successfully spark initial interest.

   - **Conversion optimization:** For conversion optimization, time-decay or data-driven attribution models are often the most effective. Time-decay models assign more credit to touchpoints closer to the conversion, recognizing that recent interactions typically have a stronger influence on the final decision. Data-driven models go further by using machine learning to analyze actual user behavior and assign credit based on the true impact of each touchpoint across the customer journey. Both approaches provide a nuanced understanding of how different channels contribute to conversions, enabling marketers to allocate budget and optimize campaigns more accurately for better results.

4. **Validate with Lift Tests:** Validating attribution insights with lift tests is a powerful way to measure the true impact of marketing channels. Lift tests involve running controlled experiments—such as A/B tests or holdout groups—where a portion of the audience is exposed to a campaign while another isn't. By comparing the behavior or conversions between these groups, marketers can isolate and quantify the incremental effect of a specific channel or tactic. This experimental approach helps confirm whether attribution models reflect real-world performance, ensuring that marketing investments are based on reliable data and driving genuine growth.

5. **Educate Stakeholders:** Educating stakeholders is essential to ensure everyone understands the strengths and limitations of attribution models and the context behind the data. By clearly communicating how attribution works, what assumptions each model makes, and where potential biases or gaps exist, teams can set realistic expectations and avoid misinterpreting results. This shared understanding fosters better collaboration, informed decision-making, and trust in the analytics process, ultimately leading to more effective marketing strategies aligned with business goals.

8. Future of Attribution: Data-Driven & AI Models

The future of marketing attribution lies in data-driven and AI-powered models, which offer more accuracy, scalability, and adaptability than traditional approaches. These advanced models use machine learning algorithms to analyze vast amounts of customer journey data, identifying patterns and assigning credit based on actual behavior rather than static rules. As privacy regulations tighten and third-party cookies phase out, AI-based attribution can rely more on first-party data, contextual signals, and probabilistic matching to track and model user interactions. Platforms like Google Analytics 4, Adobe Sensei, and Meta's Conversion API are already incorporating AI to optimize attribution insights in real time. These models continuously learn and improve, offering marketers deeper insights into what truly drives conversions, allowing for more precise targeting, budget allocation, and campaign optimization. As attribution becomes more intelligent, it will shift from being a reporting tool to a predictive engine for strategic decision-making.

Modern platforms are moving toward machine learning-powered attribution, where models:

- Use statistical analysis of user behavior.
- Learn from large datasets to assign credit dynamically.
- Adjust based on context, device type, and channel performance.

Examples:

- Google's Data-Driven Attribution (DDA)
- Facebook Conversion Lift

These models offer higher accuracy but rely on sufficient data volume and clean event tracking.

Conclusion

Attribution modeling and multi-touch analysis are essential tools in the digital marketer's toolkit. By understanding how each channel contributes to the customer journey, marketers can optimize spend, personalize messaging, and prove the true value of their efforts. In a world where every click matters, attribution ensures every click is counted — and counted right.

CHAPTER FIFTEEN

The Future of Digital Marketing Analytics

Introduction

Digital marketing analytics is evolving at an unprecedented pace. As technology, privacy expectations, and consumer behavior shift, the tools, techniques, and mindsets required to succeed in analytics must adapt. In this final chapter, we explore the trends shaping the future of digital marketing analytics and what marketers can do to stay ahead of the curve.

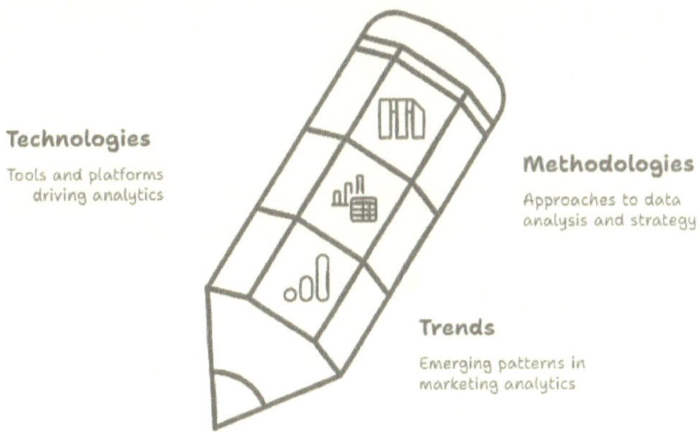

1. From Data Collection to Data Intelligence

In today's digital landscape, businesses must move beyond just gathering data—they need to transform it into actionable intelligence. The journey begins with data collection, which involves capturing information from various sources such as websites, mobile apps, social media, email campaigns, CRMs, and transaction systems. However, raw data alone holds limited value unless it is cleaned, structured, and integrated across platforms. The next phase is data analysis, where tools like Google Analytics, Looker Studio, or Power BI help uncover patterns, trends, and correlations. Finally, this analyzed data evolves into data intelligence—strategic insights that drive decisions around customer behavior, campaign effectiveness, product improvements, and market opportunities. By converting scattered data points into meaningful narratives, organizations can predict outcomes, personalize experiences, and create a competitive edge rooted in data-driven strategy.

Traditionally, analytics focused on reporting what happened. The future lies in **predicting what will happen** and **prescribing what to do next**. The shift is from:

Past	Future
Descriptive analytics	Predictive and prescriptive analytics
Channel-based tracking	Customer-centric tracking
Manual dashboards	AI-powered insights and automation

2. AI and Machine Learning Integration

The integration of Artificial Intelligence (AI) and Machine Learning (ML) is revolutionizing how marketers interpret and act on data. These technologies go beyond traditional analytics by identifying complex patterns, predicting future behaviors, and automating decision-making at scale. In digital marketing, AI and ML are used for predictive analytics, customer segmentation, personalization, content recommendations, dynamic pricing, and real-time bidding in programmatic advertising. Machine learning models continuously learn from new data, enabling smarter campaign adjustments based on performance trends. For example, tools like Google Ads Smart Bidding and Meta's Advantage+ campaigns use ML to optimize targeting and bidding in real time. As data privacy evolves and first-party data becomes more critical, AI-driven solutions help brands make sense of vast datasets while maintaining efficiency, agility, and relevance in an increasingly competitive marketplace.

Artificial intelligence is revolutionizing analytics by:

- **Predictive Modeling:** Predictive modeling leverages historical data and machine learning to anticipate customer behaviors such as future purchases, churn risk, or likelihood to convert. By analyzing patterns and trends, these models help marketers proactively tailor campaigns, personalize messaging, and allocate resources to high-value prospects or at-risk customers. Predictive insights enable more efficient targeting and improved customer retention, ultimately driving better business outcomes by focusing efforts where they're most likely to succeed.
- **Automated Insights:** Automated insights in platforms like GA4, HubSpot, and Adobe help marketers quickly identify important trends, anomalies, and performance shifts without manual data analysis. These tools use AI and machine learning to surface relevant patterns—such as sudden drops in conversion rates or emerging audience segments—allowing teams to respond faster and make data-driven decisions with greater confidence. By automating routine analysis, marketers can focus more on strategy and optimization, improving overall efficiency and effectiveness.
- **Content Personalization:** Content personalization uses AI-driven engines that analyze user behavior, preferences, and demographics to deliver tailored experiences across websites, emails, and ads. By leveraging analytics data, these systems dynamically adjust content, product recommendations, and messaging to match individual interests and needs. This personalization increases engagement, improves customer satisfaction, and drives higher conversion rates by making interactions more relevant and timely throughout the customer journey.
- **Chatbots and Virtual Analysts:** Chatbots and virtual analysts enable users to interact with data dashboards through natural language voice or chat queries. This makes accessing complex analytics more intuitive and faster, especially for non-technical stakeholders. Instead of navigating multiple reports, users can ask questions like "What were last month's top-performing campaigns?" and receive instant, clear responses. These tools improve data accessibility, encourage self-service insights, and help teams make informed decisions with greater ease and efficiency.

Example:
A marketing dashboard powered by AI flags an unusual dip in conversions, recommends testing new CTAs, and even auto-adjusts ad bidding strategies.

3. Privacy-First Analytics

Privacy-first analytics represents a shift in how organizations collect, analyze, and use data—placing user privacy and data protection at the forefront. With increasing regulations like GDPR, CCPA, and the phasing out of third-party cookies, businesses are rethinking their data strategies to ensure compliance while still gaining valuable insights. This approach emphasizes first-party data collection, anonymization, and consent-based tracking to respect user preferences and maintain trust. Tools such as Google Analytics 4, Piwik PRO, and Matomo are designed with privacy in mind, offering features like IP anonymization and data retention controls. Privacy-first analytics doesn't mean sacrificing insights—instead, it encourages more ethical, transparent data use and smarter reliance on aggregated or modeled data. By embracing this approach, brands can build credibility, safeguard user data, and still make informed, data-driven decisions.

With growing global privacy regulations (GDPR, CCPA, and others), analytics must become more ethical and compliant.

- **First-Party Data Collection:** First-party data collection is becoming increasingly important as privacy regulations and third-party cookie restrictions limit access to external data sources. This approach relies on gathering data directly from users who have given explicit consent—through websites, apps, or subscriptions—making the data more reliable and privacy-compliant. Owning first-party data allows businesses to build richer customer profiles, deliver personalized experiences, and maintain control over their marketing strategies while respecting user privacy and regulatory requirements.
- **Server-Side Tracking:** Server-side tracking shifts data collection from the user's browser to the server, reducing reliance on browser cookies that are often blocked or deleted. This method improves data accuracy and reliability by capturing interactions directly from the server, bypassing limitations like ad blockers or cookie restrictions. Server-side tracking enhances privacy compliance and helps marketers maintain better visibility into user behavior, enabling more precise measurement and attribution in today's evolving digital landscape.
- **Privacy-Safe Attribution Models:** Privacy-safe attribution models rely on aggregated or model-based data rather than tracking individual users, helping marketers comply with privacy regulations while still gaining

valuable insights. These approaches use statistical methods, machine learning, or cohort analysis to estimate channel contributions without exposing personal information. By moving away from user-level tracking, privacy-safe models protect consumer data, reduce compliance risks, and provide reliable attribution insights that balance marketing effectiveness with respect for user privacy.

Future-ready analytics must balance insight generation with respect for privacy and trust.

4. Real-Time, Cross-Channel Analysis

Real-time, cross-channel analysis empowers marketers to monitor and respond to customer behavior instantly across multiple touchpoints—such as websites, social media, email, search, and mobile apps. Instead of analyzing data in silos or after-the-fact, this approach offers a unified view of marketing performance as it happens, allowing for faster decision-making and campaign optimization. Tools like Google Looker Studio, Adobe Experience Cloud, and Power BI enable the integration of data streams from various platforms to create live dashboards that reflect current activity. This real-time insight helps teams identify trends, detect anomalies, allocate budgets dynamically, and personalize user experiences on the fly. In a fast-paced digital environment, cross-channel analysis ensures brands stay agile, data-informed, and customer-focused—turning complex data flows into competitive advantages.

Consumers interact across platforms, apps, and devices. Modern analytics must reflect that reality.

- **Unified Customer Views:** Unified customer views bring together data from CRM systems, websites, social media, advertising platforms, and offline interactions into a single, comprehensive profile. This holistic approach enables marketers to understand customers' behaviors, preferences, and journeys across all touchpoints. By breaking down data silos and connecting disparate sources, unified views empower personalized marketing, improve targeting accuracy, and provide deeper insights into customer lifetime value, ultimately driving more effective and cohesive marketing strategies.

- **Cross-Device Measurement:** Cross-device measurement tracks customer journeys seamlessly across multiple devices—such as mobile phones, desktops, tablets—and even offline interactions like in-store visits. By connecting user behavior across these channels, marketers gain a holistic understanding of how customers engage with their brand at every touchpoint. This comprehensive view improves attribution accuracy, helps optimize campaigns for multi-device experiences, and enables personalized marketing strategies that reflect real-world buying behaviors.

- **Omnichannel Dashboards:** Omnichannel dashboards provide a unified view of marketing performance across the entire customer funnel—spanning awareness, consideration, conversion, and retention—rather than focusing on isolated campaigns or channels. By aggregating data from multiple sources like social media, email, paid ads, and offline touchpoints, these dashboards help marketers see the full picture of how different efforts interact and contribute to business goals. This holistic visualization supports better strategic decision-making, budget allocation, and optimization across `the complete customer journey.

Example:

An e-commerce brand links social ad clicks, mobile app behavior, and in-store purchase data in a single customer journey map.

5. Rise of No-Code and Citizen Analysts

The rise of no-code platforms has empowered a new generation of citizen analysts—non-technical professionals who can now work with data without writing a single line of code. Tools like Google Looker Studio, Tableau, Airtable, and Power BI offer intuitive drag-and-drop interfaces, prebuilt connectors, and visual workflows that make data exploration accessible to marketers, product managers, and business leaders alike. This democratization of data removes reliance on IT or data science teams for everyday insights, fostering faster decision-making and a data-driven culture across organizations. As businesses embrace no-code tools, citizen analysts play a crucial role in turning raw data into dashboards, reports, and actionable strategies—accelerating innovation and collaboration while reducing bottlenecks in analytics processes.

The barrier to entry is lowering:

- **No-Code Tools:** No-code tools like Google Looker Studio, Power BI, and Supermetrics democratize digital marketing analytics by enabling non-technical marketers to create, customize, and visualize data reports without writing code. These platforms offer intuitive drag-and-drop interfaces, pre-built connectors, and automation features that simplify data integration and analysis. By lowering technical barriers, no-code tools empower marketers to explore insights independently, make faster decisions, and collaborate more effectively across teams.

- **Natural Language Processing (NLP):** Natural Language Processing (NLP) in digital marketing analytics allows marketers to interact with data using everyday language, asking questions like "What were our top-performing campaigns last quarter?" and receiving instant, easy-to-understand visual answers. This technology removes the need for complex queries or technical expertise, making data insights more accessible and actionable for all team members. NLP-powered tools speed up analysis, improve decision-making, and foster a data-driven culture by simplifying how users engage with analytics.
- **Embedded Analytics:** Embedded analytics integrates data and reporting capabilities directly within apps, CRMs, and business dashboards, eliminating the need to switch between separate analytics platforms. This seamless integration allows users to access real-time insights and make data-driven decisions without leaving their workflow. By bringing analytics to the point of action, embedded analytics improves efficiency, encourages adoption across teams, and ensures that insights are timely and contextually relevant.

6. Data Democratization and Collaboration

Data democratization refers to making data accessible to everyone within an organization—regardless of technical expertise—so that informed decisions can be made at all levels. This shift enables cross-functional teams like marketing, sales, product, and customer service to independently explore insights, track KPIs, and contribute to strategic outcomes. With tools like Looker Studio, Power BI, and Notion, data is no longer confined to analysts or IT departments but becomes a shared resource for collaboration. Combined with features like role-based access, real-time dashboards, and collaborative commenting, democratized data fosters transparency, agility, and team alignment. When everyone can access and understand data, organizations become more responsive, cohesive, and empowered to act on insights—turning analytics into a company-wide advantage.

Modern analytics platforms emphasize **collaboration and accessibility**, making insights available to entire teams — not just analysts.

- **Shared Dashboards:** Shared dashboards provide real-time visibility across departments by consolidating key metrics and insights into a single, accessible platform. This transparency fosters collaboration, aligns teams around common goals, and enables faster, data-driven decision-making. With everyone viewing the same up-to-date information, organizations can break down silos, improve communication, and respond more effectively to market changes or campaign performance.
- **Data Governance Tools:** Data governance tools play a critical role in maintaining accuracy, consistency, and security as data becomes more widely accessed across an organization. These tools establish policies, standards, and workflows for data management, ensuring that data is reliable, properly classified, and compliant with regulations. By implementing data governance, businesses reduce errors, prevent misuse, and build trust in their analytics, enabling teams to confidently leverage data for strategic decisions and operational excellence.
- **Self-Service BI:** Self-service BI tools empower teams to explore and analyze data independently without relying on specialized analysts or IT support. By providing intuitive interfaces, drag-and-drop functionality, and easy access to datasets, these tools enable users across departments to generate their own reports, identify trends, and answer business questions quickly. This autonomy accelerates decision-making, fosters a data-driven culture, and reduces bottlenecks, allowing organizations to respond faster to opportunities and challenges.

7. Predictive and Prescriptive Marketing

Future analytics won't just tell marketers what happened — they'll suggest what to do next.

Concept	Definition
Predictive Analytics	Uses historical data to forecast future outcomes.
Prescriptive Analytics	Recommends actions based on likely results and constraints.

Example:

An email platform predicts which customers are likely to unsubscribe and suggests alternative content or timing to retain them.

8. Analytics for Emerging Channels

As digital behavior evolves, marketers must expand their analytics capabilities to track performance across emerging channels such as voice search, smart speakers, chatbots, messaging apps, AR/VR platforms, and connected TV (CTV). These channels generate new types of interactions that traditional web analytics may not fully capture. For instance, measuring engagement on a voice assistant or a WhatsApp chatbot requires custom event tracking and conversational analytics. Similarly, platforms like TikTok, Twitch, and YouTube Shorts demand advanced metrics like watch-through rates, creator influence, and social sentiment. Specialized tools—such as Dashbot for conversational interfaces, Conviva for streaming analytics, and Emplifi or Brandwatch for social video—help brands gain deeper visibility into these newer touchpoints. As these channels continue to grow in influence, integrating their data into a centralized analytics strategy ensures a more complete view of the customer journey and enables agile marketing across the digital landscape.

As technology grows, so do the platforms that require analytics:

- **Voice Search & Assistants:** Tracking and optimizing for voice search assistants like Alexa or Siri involves a mix of indirect and strategic approaches since these platforms don't provide traditional analytics data like websites do. Key tactics include optimizing your content for natural language queries and conversational keywords that users speak rather than type. Implementing structured data (schema markup) helps voice assistants understand and feature your content in voice search results. For tracking, you can analyze changes in branded search traffic, monitor virtual assistant-related queries through platforms like Google Search Console, and use call tracking for voice-driven interactions. Additionally, investing in smart speaker skills or actions with built-in analytics can provide insights into user engagement on those devices.
- **AR/VR Experiences:** Measuring engagement in AR/VR experiences involves tracking how users interact within immersive environments, which goes beyond traditional click or pageview metrics. Key engagement indicators include session duration, frequency of use, interaction types (e.g., object manipulation, navigation paths), and completion rates of specific tasks or experiences. Advanced analytics can capture eye-tracking data, gesture usage, and emotional responses to better understand user behavior and satisfaction. By collecting and

analyzing these rich data points, marketers and developers can optimize AR/VR content, improve user experience, and demonstrate the impact of immersive campaigns on brand awareness and conversions.

- **IoT (Internet of Things):** IoT analytics involves collecting and analyzing data generated by smart devices and wearables, such as fitness trackers, smart home systems, and connected appliances. This data provides valuable insights into user behavior, preferences, and real-time conditions, enabling personalized marketing, improved product design, and proactive customer service. By integrating IoT data with other marketing analytics, businesses can create richer customer profiles, anticipate needs, and deliver highly relevant experiences. However, IoT analytics also requires strong data management and privacy practices to handle the volume and sensitivity of information collected.

- **Metaverse & Web3:** In the metaverse and Web3 environments, engagement metrics expand beyond traditional digital analytics to capture user interactions within decentralized, immersive ecosystems. Key metrics include time spent in virtual spaces, frequency of visits, social interactions, participation in events or communities, virtual asset ownership and transactions (like NFTs), and user-generated content creation. Tracking these behaviors helps brands understand how users engage with immersive experiences, measure community growth, and evaluate the impact of virtual goods and services. Because Web3 emphasizes user control and privacy, analytics often rely on on-chain data and consent-based tracking, requiring new tools and approaches to capture meaningful insights in these evolving landscapes.

9. Human Skills Will Still Matter

As analytics becomes more automated and powered by AI, human skills remain essential to interpreting data, applying insights, and making strategic decisions. While machines can process and visualize vast datasets, it's human judgment that provides context, empathy, and ethical reasoning. Skills like critical thinking, storytelling with data, domain expertise, and strategic foresight enable professionals to ask the right questions, challenge assumptions, and turn numbers into narratives that drive impact. Moreover, collaboration, communication, and curiosity help bridge the gap between technical data outputs and real-world business goals. In a world flooded with information, the ability to connect insights to action—with creativity and human intuition—will be the defining trait of effective digital leaders.

AI may enhance our capabilities, but it's humans who give data its purpose.

Despite automation and AI, human judgment remains irreplaceable. Key future-proof skills include:

- **Critical Thinking:** Critical thinking in digital marketing analytics means carefully evaluating insights to determine their relevance, accuracy, and potential biases before making decisions. It involves questioning the data sources, understanding the context in which data was collected, and recognizing limitations or assumptions within models and reports. By applying critical thinking, marketers can avoid overreliance on misleading metrics, identify false correlations, and ensure that strategies are based on meaningful, objective evidence—leading to more effective and trustworthy outcomes.

- **Data Storytelling:** Data storytelling is the art of transforming complex data and analytics into clear, compelling narratives that resonate with audiences. It combines data visualization, context, and storytelling techniques to highlight key insights, explain their significance, and connect them to business goals. Effective data storytelling helps stakeholders understand not just the "what" but the "why" behind the numbers, making it easier to drive informed decisions, build alignment, and inspire action across teams.

- **Ethical Analysis:** Ethical analysis in digital marketing analytics involves ensuring that data is collected, processed, and used responsibly—respecting user privacy, avoiding manipulation, and preventing harm. This means being transparent about data practices, obtaining informed consent, and using data in ways that are fair and non-discriminatory. Ethical analysis also requires vigilance against biased algorithms or misleading interpretations that could harm individuals or groups. By prioritizing ethics, organizations build trust with customers and stakeholders, fostering long-term relationships and sustainable business practices.

10. Preparing for the Future: Recommendations

To stay ahead in the evolving world of digital analytics, organizations must proactively prepare for a future that is more automated, privacy-conscious, and insight-driven. First, invest in scalable analytics tools that support AI integration, multi-channel tracking, and privacy-first design. Next, prioritize the collection of first-party data and build systems that ensure data quality, governance, and compliance. Equip teams with training in data literacy, empowering both technical and non-technical roles to engage with data confidently. Encourage a culture of experimentation, where data is used not only to report outcomes but to test, learn, and innovate continuously. Finally, blend technology with human expertise—use automation for efficiency, but rely on human insight for context, creativity, and ethical judgment. By aligning tools, talent, and strategy, businesses can turn today's data into tomorrow's competitive advantage.

- Invest in First-Party Data Strategies
- Adopt AI-Powered Analytics Platforms
- Train Teams in Visualization and Data Literacy
- Implement Agile Analytics Practices
- Prioritize Ethical and Transparent Reporting

Conclusion

The future of digital marketing analytics is smarter, faster, and more connected — but also more ethical, privacy-conscious, and customer-focused. As new technologies and expectations reshape the landscape, marketers must evolve from data collectors to strategic analysts and trusted advisors.

Success in tomorrow's digital world won't depend just on how much data you have — but on how intelligently, ethically, and creatively you use it.